Roots, Feathers, & Blooms:
4-Block Quilts,
Their History & Patterns
Book I

Linda Giesler Carlson

Library of Congress Cataloging-in-Publication Data

Carlson, Linda Giesler.
    Roots, feathers & blooms : 4-block quilts, their history &
patterns / Linda Giesler Carlson.
            p.   cm.
    Includes bibliographical references (p. 127) and index.
    ISBN 0-89145 -825-5 (v. 1) : $16.95
    1. Patchwork--Patterns.   2. Quilting--Patterns.   3.Patchwork
quilts--United States--History.   I Title.   II Title: Roots,
feathers, and blooms.
TT835.C374   1994
746.46--dc20   94--27580
                                                                            CIP

Additional copies of this book may be ordered from:

American Quilter's Society
P.O. Box 3290
Paducah, KY 42002-3290
@16.95. Add $1.00 for postage and handling.

Dedication

This book is dedicated to:

my dad, Frederick Herman Giesler,
who shared my joy in finding a publisher for this book
but did not live to see it published.
I share it with him in spirit.
He was always the first to say,
"We're proud of all you kids";

my grandmother, Melinda Giesler,
who unbeknownst to either of us,
planted the seed of love for quilts;

my mother, Emma Jean Lemon Giesler,
who knowingly taught me the love of sewing,
("always make the wrong side as accurate as the front")

my twin sister, Diana Henage,
who continues to stimulate my competitive spirit,
(she's already written a textbook for gifted children);

my best friend, Roslyn Dial,
who listened to me through thick and thin;

my children, Amy and Meredith,
who kept me on track with
"When's my quilt going to be done";

and last, but definitely not least,
this book is dedicated to my husband, John,
who, although he doesn't believe in collecting antique
quilts yet, does believe in me!

Love for the comfort of quilts began early with me. I loved their soul-soothing ability then and have felt a mysterious "pull" towards them since.
Myself, left; my twin sister Diana right, at 6½ months.

Table of Contents

Preface

This book could not have been done without the cooperation of many state quilt documentation project directors and museum curators. I am indebted to all of them for their words of encouragement and cooperation, especially to Emily Blair and Jeanette Lasansky of the Oral Traditions Project, Lewisburg, PA, research assistant and project director respectively; Laurel Horton, director of the South Carolina project; Bets Ramsey, co-director of the Tennessee project; and Marguerite Wiebusch, co-chair of the Indiana project book committee; and to Cheryl Wieburg Kennedy, director of the Illinois project. My sincerest gratitude goes to Meredith Schroeder and AQS for believing in this project and to Victoria Faoro, executive editor of AQS; no author could be more pleased with her expertise and friendliness than I am.

A heart felt personal thank you to a very talented quilter, Katie Borntreger. Without her speed and expertise, my quilts would still be tops! The quilts in my collection were purchased in Kalona, Iowa, with the diligent help of Marilyn Woodin, owner of Woodin Wheel Antiques, and Sara Miller, owner of Kalona Kountry Kreations. I would like to take this opportunity to thank them both for always watching for them, and notifying me ASAP!

Many of the photos included are reproductions of slides taken during documentation days held by the various state quilt searches. Since most were not selected to be reproduced by a professional photographer for the states' accompanying project books, these photographs will often include holding clips, numbers on the quilts, the quilt stand, or even documentation volunteers holding the quilts for the photographer. But each is an example of an unusual block pattern, or a quilt that wonderfully illustrates the data found.

My statistics on 4-block quilts are a compilation of data

from survey forms that were returned to me from museums and state survey projects. Kentucky was the first state to attempt a state wide quilt search, then Missouri, in the early and mid 1980's, respectively. Other states later undertaking documentation projects enjoyed the benefits of their predecessors' trail blazing quilt search efforts. My criteria stipulated that the quilts come from states that came into the Union before 1850, and were made before 1900, to include those made by state-to-state emigres.

I hope that other researchers will follow me and dig into national quilt search projects for possible trends, patterns, and threads of information leading to further knowledgeable conclusions. Many of the project directors indicated the tremendous desire and desperate need to have their information computer accessible. I couldn't agree more, and would challenge all state quilt guilds to involve local quilt guilds in grassroots efforts to help with the fund-raising such activity would require. There are a wealth of unique puzzle pieces within each state project just waiting to be seen as an integral part of a greater picture. Let's set up the table, gather the chairs, and get to work!

Coxcomb. *73" x 80". 1984. Made by Gwen Marston. Photo: The Keva Partnership.*

Introduction

Can quiltmakers turn morbid thoughts into practical thoughts? Can these morbid thoughts be an impetus to action? Since the idea of sewing snippets of fabric together to make something of practical use occurred to mankind centuries ago, the logical and only answer to these questions is an unequivocal YES! That's exactly what happened to me.

In humble awe, I attend every quilt show I possibly can, subscribe to 95% of the quilt magazines available, own a gallery of quilt books, and purchase several quilt calendars each year just to feed my insatiable habit of "quilt-a-vision."

About five years ago, I suddenly realized that I wasn't going to live long enough to make all the wonderful quilts I saw that called out, "Make ME…not the one three pages back or the one you saw at Show and Tell last week!" I had drooled over Gwen Marston and Joe Cunningham's book *American Beauties: Rose and Tulip Quilts* several times when a 4-block quilt they had made and those done by Mary Schafer and Betty Harriman spoke to me: "We have only four blocks! Think how many of us you can make in the time it would take you to finish a 30 or more block quilt!" My morbid realization that I might not live 125 years was no longer such a problem. With only four blocks per quilt, I could make all the lovely patterns I yearned to try! True, each block would be 25 inches to 45 inches square, but the appliqué pieces would be large. Eureka! My dilemma was solved.

You, too, can finish more quilts with appliquéd or pieced patterns by enlarging your favorites to fit a 4-block setting, or by starting with the six patterns provided in this book. I have included original variations of the four most popular 4-block patterns plus two one-of-a-kind special patterns.

If you love appliqué, the borders for your 4-block can be undulating vines with floral motifs from the blocks or you can use a reverse appliqué motif with an appliquéd Dogtooth border to simulate a pieced and appliquéd border. You can also use a large floral fabric for the borders and quilt around selected flowers to give your quilt an Early American look. For those of you who prefer quilting to appliquéing or piecing, the 4-block set provides ample space for background quilting, designs between appliqué pieces, or large motifs and sprays of quilting designs.

Upon viewing the photo gallery of quilts, it is my hope that you will begin to itch with anticipation to start stitching your personal rebuttal to being a mortal quiltmaker!

LOOKING BACKWARD BEGS QUESTIONS

Does history repeat itself or not? It certainly does if you've become a quilter since the early 1970's. When the 20th century 4-block quilts in Gwen Marston and Joe Cunningham's *American Beauties* caught my eye, I wrote to Gwen to purchase the booklet accompanying the Mary Schafer Quilt Collection exhibit she had curated for the Whaley Historical Home in Flint, Michigan. About the same time, I read magazine articles on the Rose Kretsinger Collection at the Spencer Art Museum in Lawrence, Kansas, and the quilts made by Charlotte Jane Whitehill. Kretsinger's 4-block 1927 Pride of Iowa absolutely took my breath away! Further digging through all my books, magazines, and calendars for 4-block quilts produced an enigma. I found more 19th century 4-block quilts than 20th century ones, but the patterns and colors hadn't changed much with one exception: the addition of the Sunbonnet Sue pattern in 1920's and 1930's pastel colors.

The common threads between the two centuries' 4-block quilts were: (1) the flower-filled urns, Princess Feather, Whig Rose, and Tree of Life patterns and; (2) the color choices of red and green, bright pinks, yellows, and blues. Considering the given dates of construction and provenance led me to wonder if this style/setting had naturally evolved after the whole-cloth quilt and medallion styles and before the multi-block quilt, and if the patterns

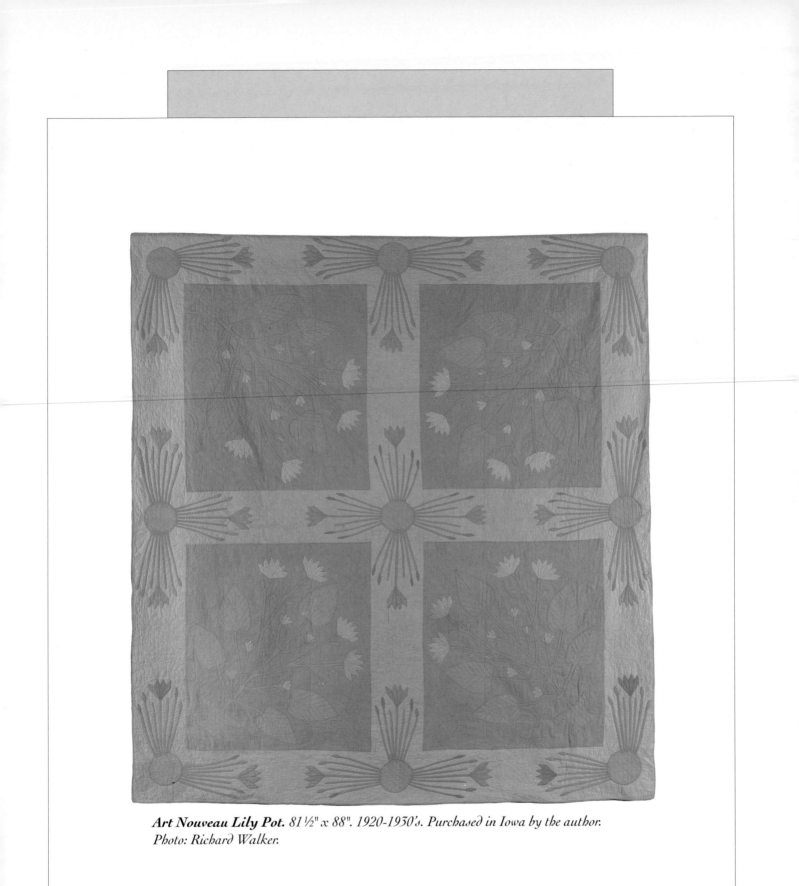

Art Nouveau Lily Pot. *81½" x 88". 1920-1930's. Purchased in Iowa by the author.*
Photo: Richard Walker.

and settings had come from a particular ethnicity. Suddenly the elementary school teacher in me took over. If I was going to teach a subject I knew little about, I was going to have to do some research. In 1988, I scratched the surface of disjointed and scarce information to write a short lecture and purchase slides of museum and private collections in time to give a hands-on workshop.

When I discovered the American Quilt Study Group's 1992 Symposium was to be held in Lincoln, NE, I realized I could drive to the conference. By 1990-91, many state quilt search projects had collected a wealth of information on their documentation forms. I was sure this was the definitive place to start for serious research, and as a testament and tribute to the unselfish work of the thousands of volunteer documentors, this book would not have been possible without those state projects.

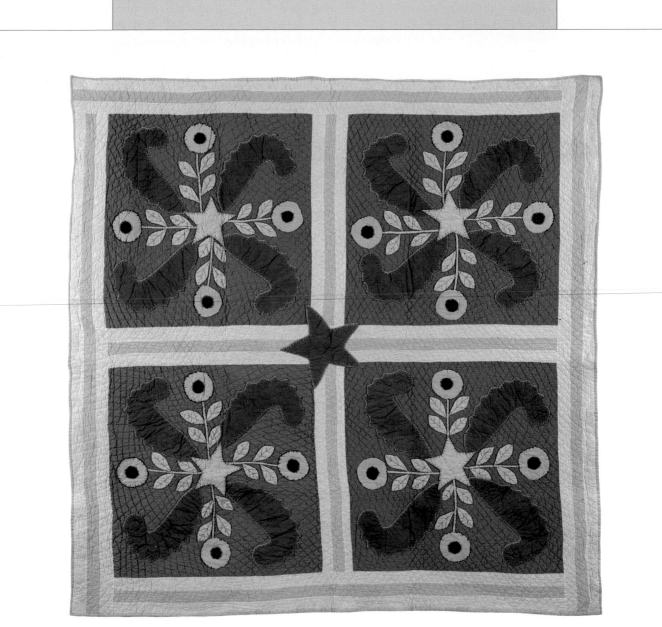

Hettie's Washington Plume. *74" x 86". 1928-32.*
Made by Hettie McBride Campbell. Documentation forms from
Florida revealed no 19th century 4-block quilts and only this one
20th century quilt, which didn't fit my criteria, but it seems appro-
priate to include a few 20th century quilts because it was the 20th
century 4-block quilts that led me to research their origins in the
19th century. Owned by Charlotte Freels Duvall.
Photo: Richard Walker.

Charlotte & Hettie

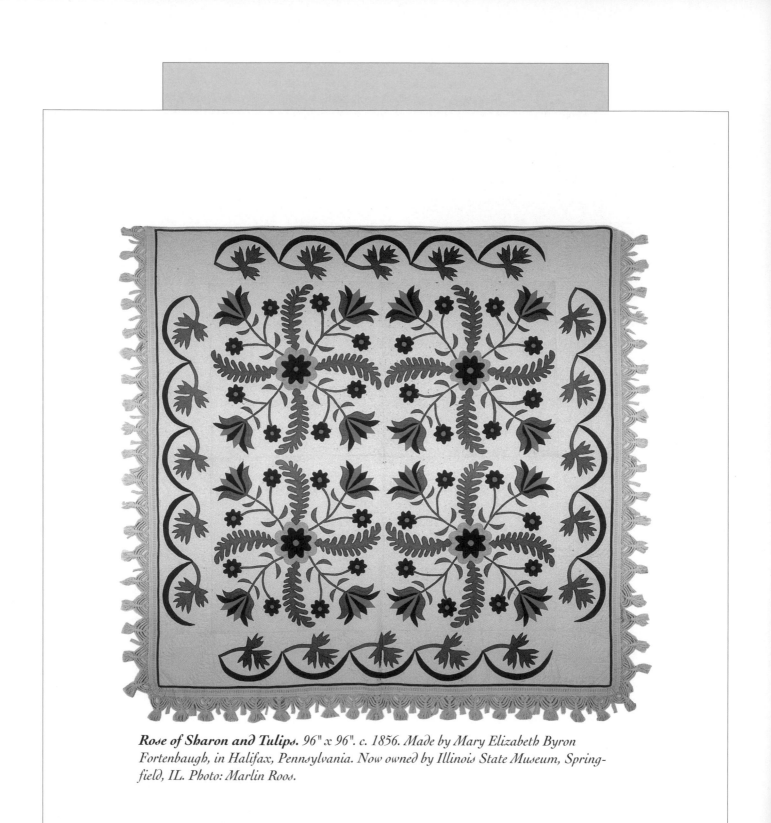

Rose of Sharon and Tulips. *96" x 96". c. 1856. Made by Mary Elizabeth Byron Fortenbaugh, in Halifax, Pennsylvania. Now owned by Illinois State Museum, Springfield, IL. Photo: Marlin Roos.*

Chapter 1
4-Block Quilt Designs
& Their Origins

Four patterns are most commonly used in 4-block quilts: Princess Feather, Whig Rose, Flower Filled Urns, and Tree of Life. While they have all enjoyed template variations over their 170 year use, they are still readily recognizable patterns.

Tulip Designs

One of the designs frequently found on quilts made during the blossoming of 4-block quilts in America had its roots one ocean, half a continent, and three centuries away. Turkey provided sixteenth-century Europe with tulips, one of the flowers that would eventually grow on 4-block quilts. Single bulbs commanded enormous prices during the "tulip-mania" of the 1630's.[1]

Women wanting to bring a little of their homeland with them packed a few bulbs among their belongings when emigrating to America – or paid dearly for them when the merchant ship arrived. Well suited to the climates of the northern colonies, tulips became Holland's lucrative export to America in the 1700's. Women grew these colorful flowers and also preserved them for posterity in their hearts, their minds, and their quilts.

The tulip as a quilt design became especially popular with Pennsylvania and South Carolina German quiltmakers, who depicted this flower as often or perhaps even more often than the ever-popular rose. Pfalz, now in the state of Rhineland-Pfalz in Bavaria, was the homeland of many immigrants who arrived in Philadelphia. From the Rhine, Baden, and Wurttemberg states of Germany, came many immigrants who settled in the Dutch Fork area of South Carolina.[2] In these areas Fraktur decoration adorned legal documents, such as birth, wedding, and death certificates; and these designs became popular motifs for pictorial embroidery and weaving. Fraktur painting embellished furniture, wedding chests, and decorated ceramics, and painted hex signs above barn doors protected the farm animals from witches' spells or the feared "evil eye."

Bulbous tulips with pointed petals were one of the motifs from Fraktur most often used in quiltmaking. Hearts, vines, perched birds, facing or kissing birds (especially on a wedding quilt), astronomical objects, and the round, colorful hex signs with simple floral or geometric designs were used as well, often executed in the favored colors of red, yellow, blue, and green.

A very common way to display tulips on quilts was to place these flowers and a variety

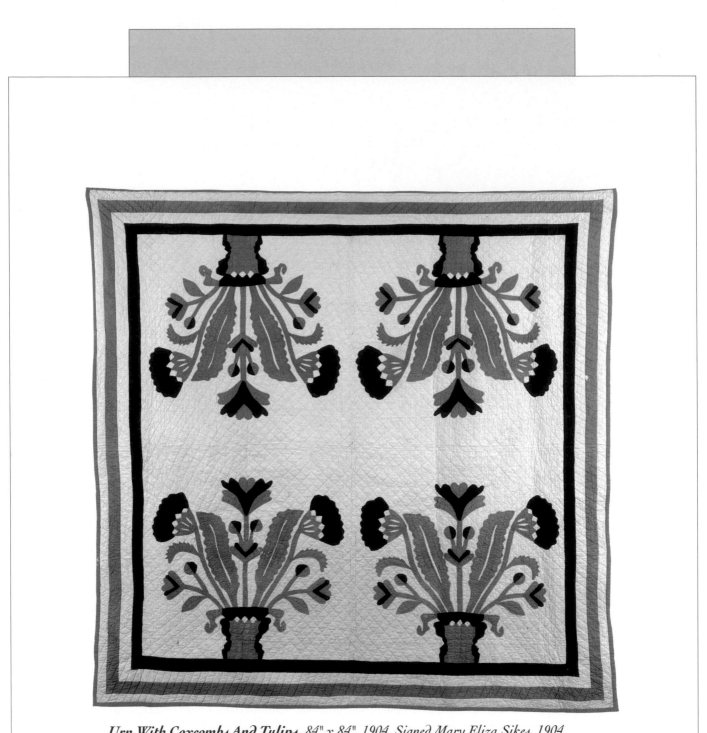

Urn With Coxcombs And Tulips. *84" x 84". 1904. Signed Mary Eliza Sikes, 1904.*
Purchased in Iowa by the author. Photo: Richard Walker.

Urn With Flowers And Currants. *84" x 84". 1840. Made by Lavina Frick, born 1827. She completed this quilt when she was 13 years old. (Note the piping next to the binding.) Author's collection. Photo: Richard Walker.*

Lavina Frick

Aumiller County Red and Gray Prince's Feather.
87" x 87". c. 1900. Made by wife of Colonel Henry Royer,
(Rebersburg). Photo: Oral Traditions Project, Lewis-
burg, PA.

His Royal Highness Prince of Wales Insignia.

of others in an urn or vase. Several state quilt documentation projects found 4-block urn quilts filled with tulips, roses, coxcombs, currants, and cherries.

PRINCESS FEATHER DESIGNS

The pattern we today call Princess Feather, often appearing in a 4-block setting, may have originally been named the Prince's Feather or the Prince of Wales Feather. In 1301, King Edward I of Great Britain invested his son, the future Edward II, with the title Prince of Wales. Each succeeding eldest son was likewise invested before accepting the British Crown. C. Stevens, curator of Welsh Folk Museum in Wales relates, "According to the *Oxford Companion to Welsh Literature*, the motto of the Prince of Wales, 'Ich Dien,' (German for *I serve*) ... together with the three white ostrich feathers ... form the Prince's Insignia...."

The Prince's Feather insignia, which is still used today, was first depicted on drawings and paintings as three feathers spewing above but attached to the center of a crown worn by the Prince. Artist Robert Peake immortalized Henry, Prince of Wales, in about 1610, wearing such a triple plumed headdress.[3]

About the Prince of Wales Feathers quilt pattern, C. Stevens, comments further, "This is not a motif which figures in Welsh quilting. It is a royal motif pertaining to the Prince of Wales, and is, I believe, Germanic in origin, having no Welsh significance whatsoever!" After 1714 when German George I ascended to the British throne, German decorative goods found their way to the colonies as a result of the English Navigation Acts.[4] In the last quarter of the 19th century, Franklin

Prince of Wales Feathers and Crown. *28" x 28". Made by the author.*
This quilt block was inspired by the Aumiller County, PA, Red and Gray Prince's Feather
quilt found by the Oral Traditions Project. The pattern for this quilt is featured on
page 42. Photo: Richard Walker.

Princess Feather with Swag Bud Border. *83" x 100". c. 1870-90.*
Music may have been very important to the maker. Harps can be found in the quilting.
Purchased in Iowa by the author. Photo: Richard Walker.

Jester's Plume / Princess Feather. *83" x 83". c. 1860-80. Indiana.*
This may have been a wedding quilt as it has numerous hearts in the quilting. Author's
collection. Photo: Richard Walker.

College of Pennsylvania was established to educate Germans in English culture and taste.[5]

"Soldier's Plume" was found by the Kentucky Quilt Project and featured two feathers arcing away from a central flower. Considering these various feather patterns and their names, Jonathan Holstein, quilt scholar and author, has designated the set of triple feathers as Prince of Wales Feathers and the single running feather spray as the Princess Feather. Conversations with Welsh quiltmakers have confirmed this distinction.

ROSE DESIGNS

The rose, originating in Japan and China, made its way to England and France via trade ships as early as medieval times. Rose varieties were depicted on wool tapestries of the Middle Ages and adorned the glazed and unglazed cotton chintzes that were made in England and France and imported to the American colonies.

During the mid-eighteenth and nineteenth centuries, rose patterned chintzes were stitched to backings or cut out and appliquéd on linen or cotton to create early American whole-cloth and medallion style quilts. The North Carolina project found many fine examples of these quilts.

As these styles faded in popularity and the repeated block quilt dominated, roses never failed to bloom. Many rose patterns continued to be found on quilts, particularly those made by women of English or Scots-Irish heritage. Rainfall almost every day of the rose growing season in the United Kingdom gave birth to the still celebrated English rose gardens. Colonials and later immigrants appliquéd them on their "new garden beds." The most popular 4-block rose pattern was the Whig Rose.

Harrison Rose and Tulip Appliqué. c. 1860-1875. Made in Pennsylvania. Owned by Patricia Cox, Minneapolis, Minnesota. Photo: Patricia Cox.

Other Flower Designs

Even flowers considered weeds in some countries found their way to 4-block quilts. The Thistle pattern came from Scotland, where it was a royal insignia, created in 1452 by James II for men inducted into knighthood. The K.T. initials after their names meant "Knight of the Thistle." This woody, prickly scrub plant is extremely hearty and tenacious, and stands for unity and pride. Women of Scots heritage remembered this symbol of courage and tenacity in the face of adversity by stitching it on their quilts in a new land.

Although not seen often, the ancient Egyptian Lotus pattern looks very akin to the thistle and is often confused with it. Another flower similar to the thistle is the coxcomb, which was often found in urns or vases in the large 4-block quilts. Both the Lotus and Coxcomb patterns could well be variations of the Thistle. I have found these three names to be interchangeable on very similar 4-block quilts and printed patterns.

Tree of Life Designs

The other popular 4-block pattern found with some regularity is the Tree of Life design. This pattern first emerged as a chintz central medallion motif in the mid-eighteenth to the mid-nineteenth centuries. Several of these Tree of Life medallion quilts were found by the North Carolina quilt documentation project. When created in the 4-block set, the Tree of Life motif is not quite as elaborate in leaf, flower, fruit, or bird as its medallion predecessor, and instead of chintzes solid and print calicoes were used to create the trees and other motifs.

Pieced Designs

Very few pieced 4-block quilts have been found in state documentation projects. South Carolina documented more pieced 4-block quilts than any other state in my survey. All were made in the last quarter of the nineteenth century, and most often four stars were depicted. Blazing Star was a common pattern, although several eight-pointed stars were seen. Some pieced 4-block quilt patterns such as the Carolina Lily pattern included a small amount of appliqué. Rocky Mountain pattern quilts were also found, and two quilts featured four large X's. Only rarely did some pieced original patterns surface, but a few that did are spectacular, like the Missouri quilt in Chapter 2 and the Illinois example in Chapter 4.

Thistles In Urn. *c. 1843-1868. Made in Guntersville, Alabama, and documented by the Alabama Decorative Arts Survey, Birmingham Museum of Art. The author's collection of 4-block patterns includes two commercially printed thistle patterns very similiar to this quilt. Photo: Pat Kyser.*

San Juan Island Thistle.
Photo: John V. Carlson.

Pot of Coxcomb. *80" x 84". c. 1860-80. Indiana. Purchased in Iowa by the author.*
Photo: Richard Walker.

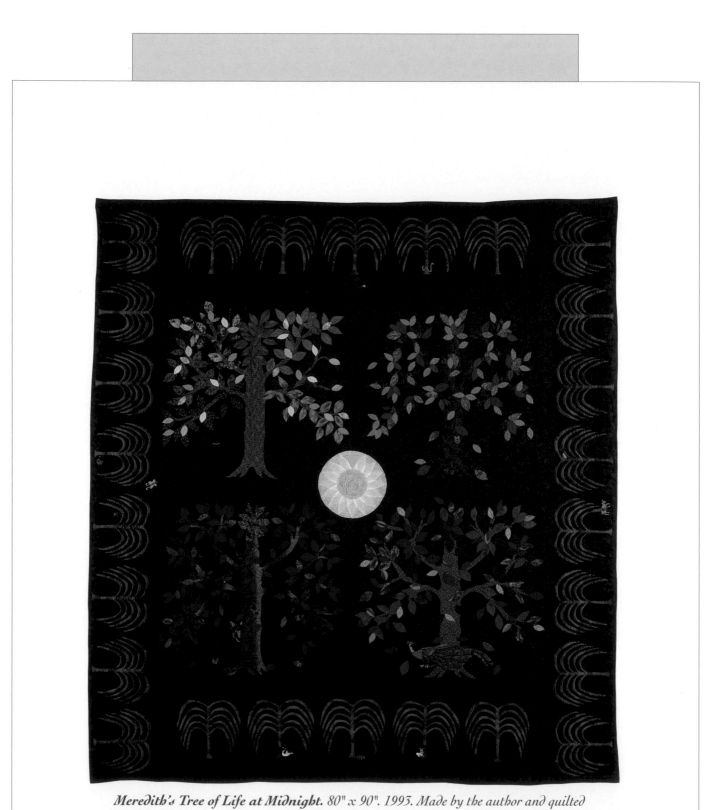

Meredith's Tree of Life at Midnight. *80" x 90". 1993. Made by the author and quilted by Katie Borntreger. The pattern for this quilt is shown on page 47. Photo: Richard Walker.*

Chapter 2
A Gallery of 4-Block Quilts

The 4-block quilts shown in this gallery are wonderful examples of the stunning results that can be achieved when this large block format is used.

Cut-out Appliqué, detail. 72½" x 76". c. 1855. Made by Martha Puralee Simmons Burton. Quilt includes reverse appliqué. Owned by Peggy Craig. Photo: Courtesy of The Quilts of Tennessee.

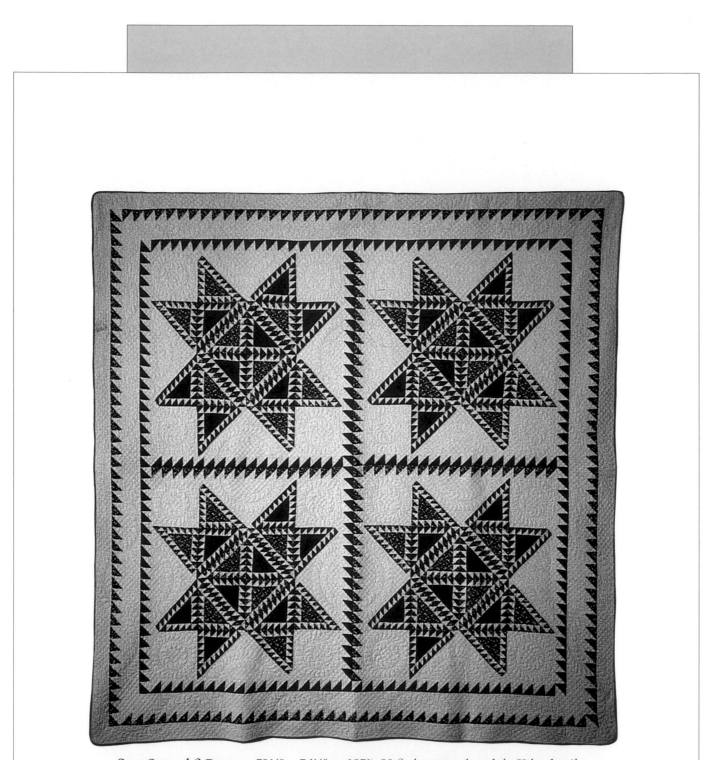

Star Spangled Banner. *72½" x 74½". c. 1875. Made by a member of the Veley family of Bowling Green, OH. This stunning red, white, and blue 4-block Star Spangled Banner quilt owned by an aunt of Ohio resident Anita Shackelford represents a numerical nightmare — perhaps that is why one seldom finds such quilts!*

Prince's Feather Variation. *86" x 86". 1860. Made by Sarah Ann Drake Terry. (Family name is Princess Feather.) This quilt was made in Ohio, but documented by the California Heritage Quilt Project and shown in their accompanying book,* Ho! For California. *Courtesy of CHQP. Owner Shirley A. Estrada. Photo: Sharon Risedorph and Lynn Kellner, San Francisco, CA.*

Pineapple Appliqué. *75" x 75". 1840. Made in South Carolina; purchased by the author in Iowa. Pencil lines on quilting still visible; never been washed. Quilted with Double Clamshell pattern. Photo: Richard Walker.*

Kentucky Tobacco Leaf and Tulip Stencil Quilt. *74" x 77½". Mid 1800's.*
Made in Kentucky, purchased in Iowa. Author's collection. Photo: Richard Walker.

Appliqué Quilt. *82" x 92". c. 1861. Made by Jennie Cleland of Pennsylvania. Owned by Jonathan Holstein, New York. Photo credit: J. Lasansky.*

Sunburst Star. 71" x 65". 1880.
*Made in Missouri and documented by Missouri Heritage
Quilt Project. Private Collection.*

Eagle. 73" x 74". 1884. Made by Mrs. Oberdorf,
*great-grandmother of Mary Koons. Photo: Oral Tradi-
tions Project, Lewisburg, PA.*

Love Apple, folded. *78½" x 89". 1870's. Back of quilt is made of meal sacks from Turner and Oates store in Mobile, Alabama. Regional lore states that the Pomegranate or Love Apple is the sliced version of a whole pineapple while other areas claim the beloved common tomato as the Love Apple. Documented by Alabama Project. Owned by Carlen House, Mobile, Alabama. Photo: Alabama Decorative Arts Survey 1549, Birmingham Museum of Arts.*

Cut-Out. *70¾" x 70¾". The border looks as if the pattern had been cut like snowflakes holding hands. Photo: Oral Traditions Project, Lewisburg, PA.*

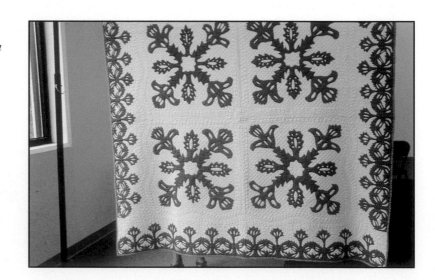

Poppy. *84" x 84". Four 33" blocks. Photo: Oral Traditions Project, Lewisburg, Pennsylvania.*

Whig Rose. *89" x 90". 1850. Made in Pennsylvania. Collection of Mary Schafer, Michigan. Photo: The Keva Partnership.*

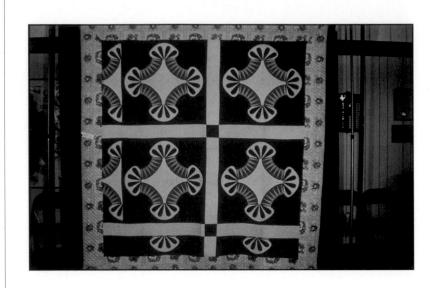

Whig's Defeat. c. 1870. Made by Sarah Adeline Stewart. Her father came to Charleston in 1788, from Belfast, Ireland, as an infant. The family settled in upper South Carolina with other Scots-Irish immigrants where they farmed and ran a saw mill. Several quilts found by the survey may be classified as "Transitional" because of their changing style, as evidenced by the chintz border in this quilt, their lengthening of a 4-block square quilt to a rectangle by adding two half blocks. None of the state projects or museums reported any 4-block x 2 half block or 6-block quilts made prior to their 4-block quilts. Collection of the McKissick Museum, The University of South Carolina. Photo: All rights reserved, McKissick Museum, The University of South Carolina.

Pineapple. 74" x 73". c. 1870. Made by Ann Smith, Richland County, SC. Two similar quilts were found in Greenville County. Collection of the McKissick Museum, The University of South Carolina. Photo: All rights reserved, McKissick Museum, The University of South Carolina.

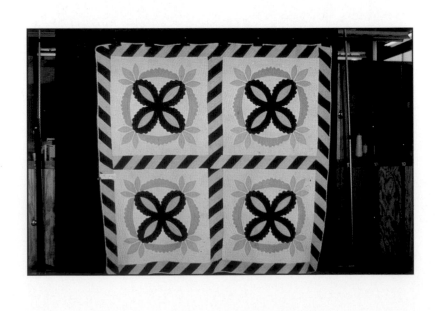

Egyptian Design. *78" x 79¼".*
Made in Pike County, Alabama. Collec-
tion of Pike Pioneer Museum. Photo:
Alabama Decorative Arts Survey, 1461,
Birmingham Museum of Art.

Rocky Mountain, detail. *75" x 77".*
c. 1880-1890. Collection of McKissick
Museum, The University of South Car-
olina. Photo: All rights reserved,
McKissick Museum, The University of
South Carolina.

Coxcomb Crossing, block. *42" x 42". Made by the author.*
This large block was inspired by an antique multi-block quilt owned by the Audrain County Historical Society Museum in Mexico, MO. It was donated by Miss Virginia Botts, whose ancestors came from Kentucky. A very similar quilt was found by the Kentucky Quilt Project. I have named it "Coxcomb Crossing" as it has previously been called "Unknown" by Barbara Brackman, author of Encyclopedia of Applique. *The pattern for this block is shown on page 60. Photo: Richard Walker.*

Whig-Harrison Rose, block. *35" x 35". Made by the author.*
The pattern for this block is shown on page 72. Photo: Richard Walker.

Princess Feather. *102" x 102". 1992. Made by the author. Quilted by Katie Borntreger. Pattern for this quilt shown on page 77. Photo: Richard Walker.*

Chapter 3
Full-size Patterns for
Large Block & 4-Block Quilts

The patterns presented in this book reflect two outstanding quilts I found during my research, as well as examples of the four most commonly found 4-block quilt designs. All of these designs are my original interpretations, with the exception of "Cox-comb Crossing," which is a slightly changed reproduction of an unnamed antique quilt.

Both piecing and appliqué techniques are used in the six patterns, which are geared to the intermediate to advanced quiltmaker. Some patterns such as "Amy's Wedding Quilt" require piecing in certain sections of the block. "Coxcomb Crossing" is probably the most challenging of the patterns. It is entirely pieced and requires some curved

piecing of leaves to background pieces. The design is then appliquéd onto the background block.

Before you begin making your own 4-block quilt, prewash and iron all fabrics. Be sure to position and draw around piecing templates on the wrong side of the fabric while remembering to trace around the appliqué templates on the right side of the fabric. I find the needle-turn method of appliqué the easiest and quickest for me.

You are about to embark on an exciting project. It can be rich in symbolism or simply a decorative heirloom to pass on to future generations. And remember…there are only four blocks!

PRINCE OF WALES FEATHERS AND CROWN
28" x 28" finished size

FABRIC REQUIREMENTS
- 1 yd. background fabric
- ½ yd. for feathers
- 9" square for star
- 12" square for crown
- (4) 4" x 3" scraps for leaves
- Optional: Acrylic yarn for trapunto stems on feathers, leaves, and crown, yarn needle

BASIC SEWING KIT
- 1 large sheet template plastic
- Fabric scissors
- Template cutting scissors
- Appliqué needle
- Threads to match fabrics
- Fabric pencil

Make templates and trace around them on right side of fabric for appliquéing. Add seam allowance to fabric pieces when cutting.

CUTTING INSTRUCTIONS
- Cut (1) 28½" square for background
- Cut (1) piece A for crown
- Cut (1) piece B for star, be sure to mark top of star on template
- Cut (4) pieces C for leaves
- Cut (3) pieces D for feathers

BLOCK ASSEMBLY (Patterns: pages 44–46)
- Position crown (A) in bottom right corner of background block about 1 inch inside the bottom and side edges. Pin.
- Position and pin star (B) so that the bottom point fits under the top left corner of the crown. (See diagram, page 43.)
- Pin leaves to four star points as shown.
- Position and pin three feathers on remaining star points.
- Appliqué feathers first by needle turning under edges so that marking lines do not

show. Clip inner and outer curves where necessary, cutting through the marking lines. This will ensure smooth feather edges as well as narrow spacing between feathers. Option: Stitch ½" wide channels for stems on feathers and leaves. Stitch circular channels to resemble jewels on crown. Insert yarn from the back side.

- Appliqué star. Points should just touch bottom spines of feathers, not overlap. Cut into right angles between points to insure a smooth turn under. Turn under raw edge on pencil line. Sew up to pencil line star tip and take two stitches to hold it down while you needle turn the folded raw edge underneath the star point and back towards the sewn edge. Once the raw edge is stuffed under and away from the star point, you can continue to needle turn under the star sides. Take two appliqué stitches in those inner angles to keep raw edge from raveling.
- Appliqué leaves, starting on a side, at least an inch away from bottom of leaf. As you work towards the star point, needle turn the leaf edge in the same manner as the star point. Allow the bottom leaf point to barely touch the star point.
- Appliqué edges of crown, allowing top left section to touch bottom point with a slight overlap. Clip curves and inner angles as necessary.

Full Quilt Diagram

Fig. 1

Clip inner corner.

2 Stitches to anchor angle.

A

Pattern Guide

A
CROWN

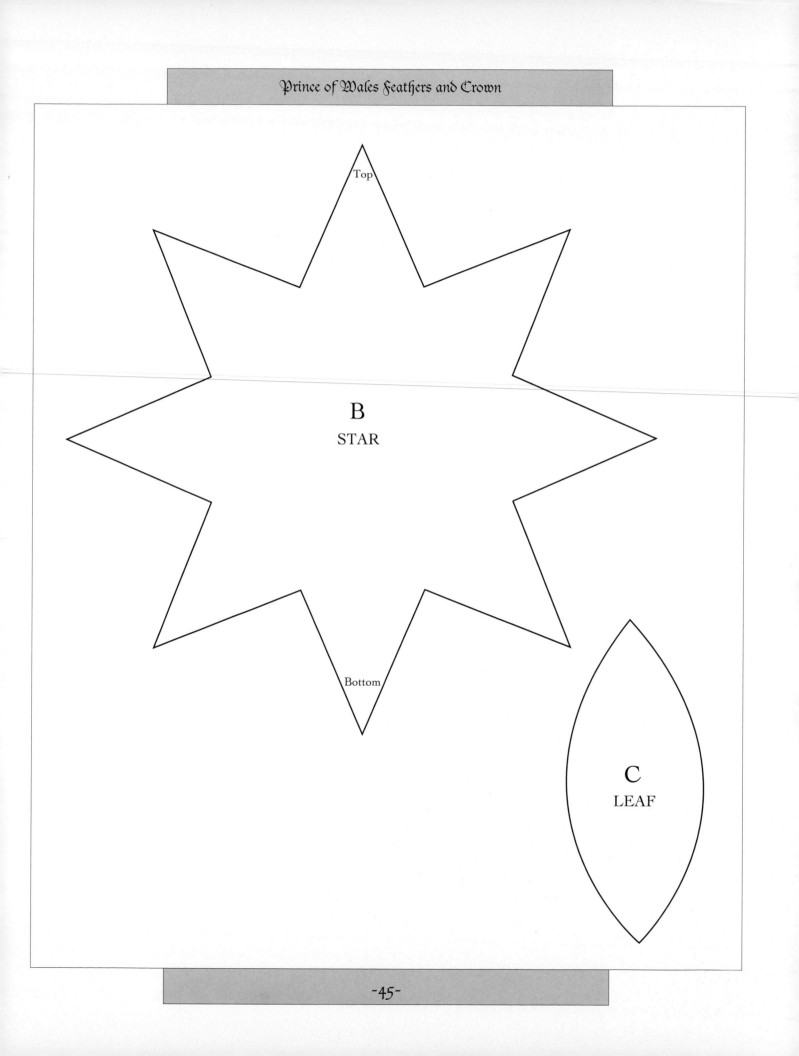

Top

B
STAR

Bottom

C
LEAF

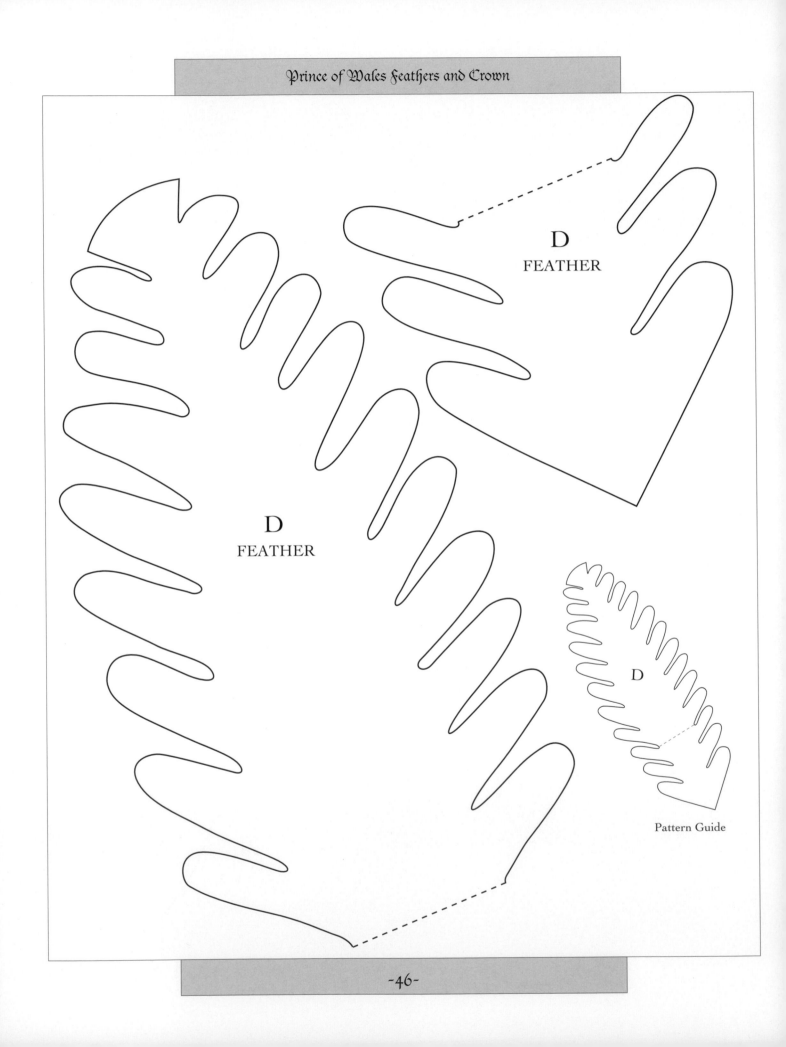

D
FEATHER

D
FEATHER

D

Pattern Guide

MEREDITH'S TREE OF LIFE AT MIDNIGHT
80" x 90" finished size

FABRIC REQUIREMENTS
   8¾ yd. for background fabric, borders,
      and binding
   ¾ yd. each for four different tree trunks
   3 yd. weeping willow fabric
   8–10 scrap colors for leaves,
      color coordinate with each tree trunk
   Scrap pieces for animals
   Scrap pieces for moon and (1) 12" square
   Batting yardage for 80" x 90" quilt
   Backing fabric yardage for 80" x 90" quilt

BASIC SEWING KIT
   2 large sheets of paper at least 24" long or equivalent sheets taped together
   Template plastic
   Fabric scissors
   Template cutting scissors
   Appliqué needle
   Threads to match fabrics
   Embroidery thread for eyes, nose, etc.
   Fabric pencil
   Optional: 130 yd. craft yarn to stuff weeping willow and a yarn needle

Tape 2 large sheets of paper together. Trace tree onto paper and cut out. Make other templates for the animals and the moon from the plastic.

CUTTING INSTRUCTIONS
   • Cut (4) 30½" blocks of background color
   • Cut (2) 10½" x 90½" borders of background color
   • Cut (2) 15½" x 60½" borders of background color
   • Cut (4) trees of different colors

- Cut (26) weeping willow trees
- Using four leaf shapes, cut four of each shape, using 8–10 color coordinated scraps for each tree trunk.
- Make as many animals as you want with scraps that resemble their plumage, fur, shells, scales, etc. I found the lark and peacock in a Jenny Beyer chintz fabric. (No pattern pieces are given for them.)
- Center moon: Trace templates on wrong side of fabric, adding seam allowance.
  Cut (1) piece A
  Cut (16) pieces B
  Cut (16) pieces C, mark top of diamond with a dot
  Cut (16) pieces D

BLOCK ASSEMBLY (Patterns pages 52–59)

Instructions are for one block.

- Position and pin tree in center of block. Pin any animals in place that need to be partially hidden by the trunk or branches now, before appliquéing tree.
- Pin scrap leaves either in a random color scheme or like colors on one branch. Pin some so they are in the midst of falling to the ground, while others lay around the tree. Appliqué down. Add all embroidery details to animals, being very careful not to pull the threads too tight, as this may cause the block to pucker out of shape.
- Option: leave the backs of some of the leaves intact by not cutting away the background fabric inside the leaf appliqué line. Instead, using that leaf's template, cut a piece of batting the size of the leaf. Carefully snip the background fabric long enough to needle stuff the leaf batt inside the leaf appliqué. See Fig. 1. This will make the leaf puff-up on the front. Baste the slit closed.

QUILT CENTER

- Join all four blocks.
- Piece center moon. Draw a tiny dot to indicate the top of diamond C on the fabric. Piece B to C, then C to D. Make all 16 units, then join together. See Fig. 2.

Fig. 1

Fig. 2

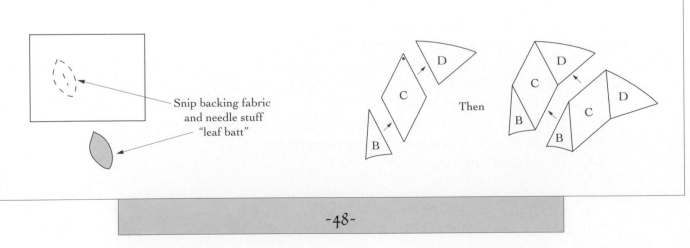

Snip backing fabric
and needle stuff
"leaf batt"

Then

- To piece center A, work with wrong side of pieced moon toward you, as if setting a sleeve into a jacket. Pin A to moon in quarter sections: north, south, east, and west. Evenly pin remaining fabric. Sew together on pencil line.
- Finger press under edges of moon on pencil line. Center over juncture where the four blocks meet. Appliqué. Cut out background fabric behind the moon, ¼" away from stitching line.

BORDERS (Position willows evenly.)

- Appliqué eight weeping willows to the long side borders. If any animals are supposed to be partially hidden by branches, pin them in place before sewing willows. Appliqué five willows to short borders.
- Option: Instead of cutting away background backing behind the willows, snip an opening ¼" above the bottom of the trunk backing. Thread yarn into yarn needle and insert into trunk opening. Snip an opening near the top of the willow and pull the yarn through, leaving a ⅜" yarn tail at the base of the trunk and another at the top of the willow. Hint: leave the yarn doubled on the needle when stuffing the trunk. Use only a single yarn when stuffing the branches. See Fig. 3 trunk.
- See Fig. 3 branches. Before stuffing branches, make a slit at the tip, middle, and base of the branch. Start threading at tip of branch leaving a ⅜" tail exposed. Stuff to middle slit bringing the needle completely out of the tunnel. Pull the yarn through. Re-insert the needle and continue threading to the base slit. Pull yarn through and cut it leaving a ⅜" tail. This midway re-insertion helps prevent the border from puckering. This puckering can be substantial enough to make the border too short to piece to the four blocks. Be very careful!

Fig. 3

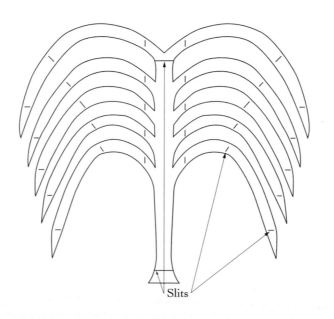

Slits

FINISHING THE QUILT

- Baste quilt top, batting, and backing after drawing quilting lines. I randomly followed the patterns on the trees and traced around the leaf templates on the background fabric. The moon has gradually increasing glow lines radiating outward to the trees. Some appliquéd leaves have quilting lines down the center. Other leaves are outline quilted, as are the weeping willows and animals.

I made this quilt for my youngest daughter, Meredith. By nature she is an animal lover, conservationist, and environmentalist. Her favorite animal is the wolf, and the weeping willow is her favorite tree. Initially, these two were included in the quilt only because she loved them so. On April 1, 1993, the weeping willows on the quilt reverted to their traditional symbolism of deep sorrow. My dad, Frederick H. Giesler, suddenly passed away. In the somber weeks that followed, I did what many have done before me to soothe their sorry souls – I quilted. Tucked under the loving arms of a weeping willow is his quilted tombstone. There on the back of the quilt is his name, birth, and final resting date. The other borders contain pairs of tombstones for my grandparents with their information recorded on the back also. All quilts have a story.

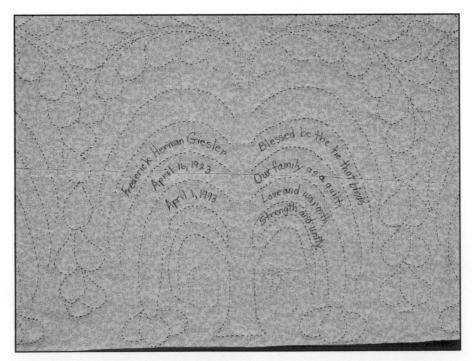

Tree of Life at Midnight, back detail. 80" x 90". 1993. Made by the author.
Photo: Richard Walker.

Full Quilt Diagram

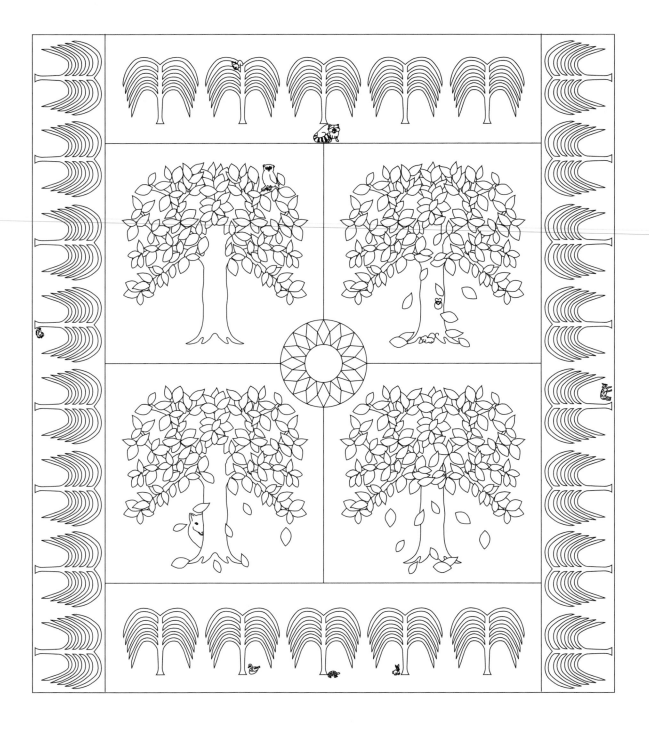

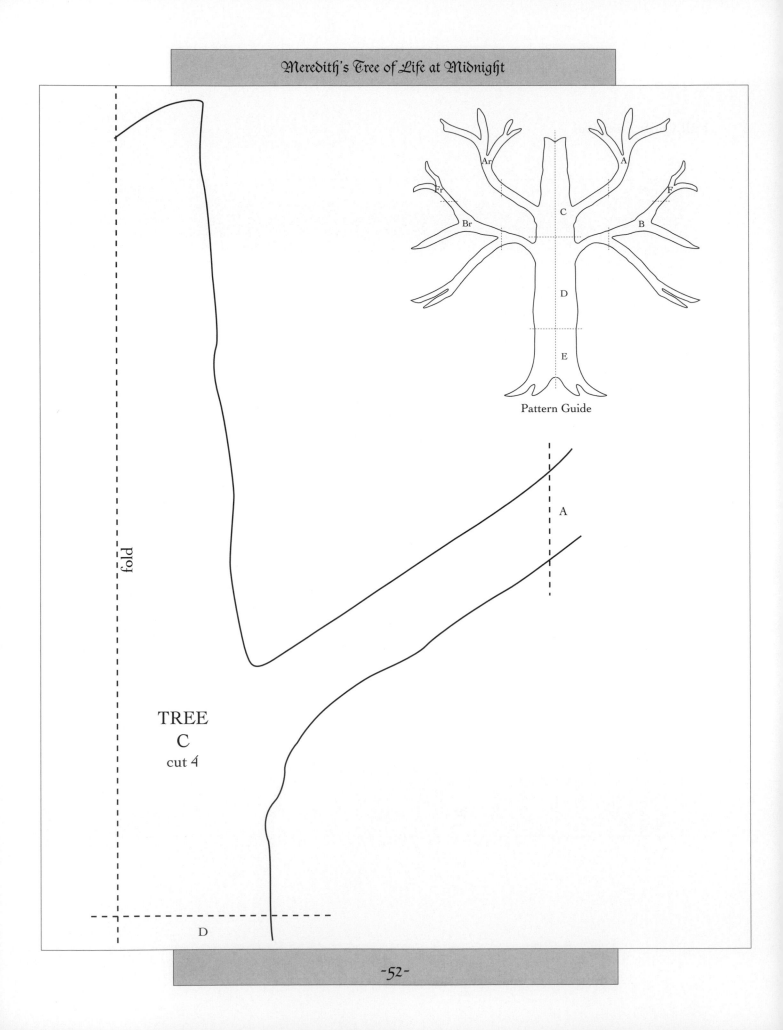

Pattern Guide

fold

A

TREE
C
cut 4

D

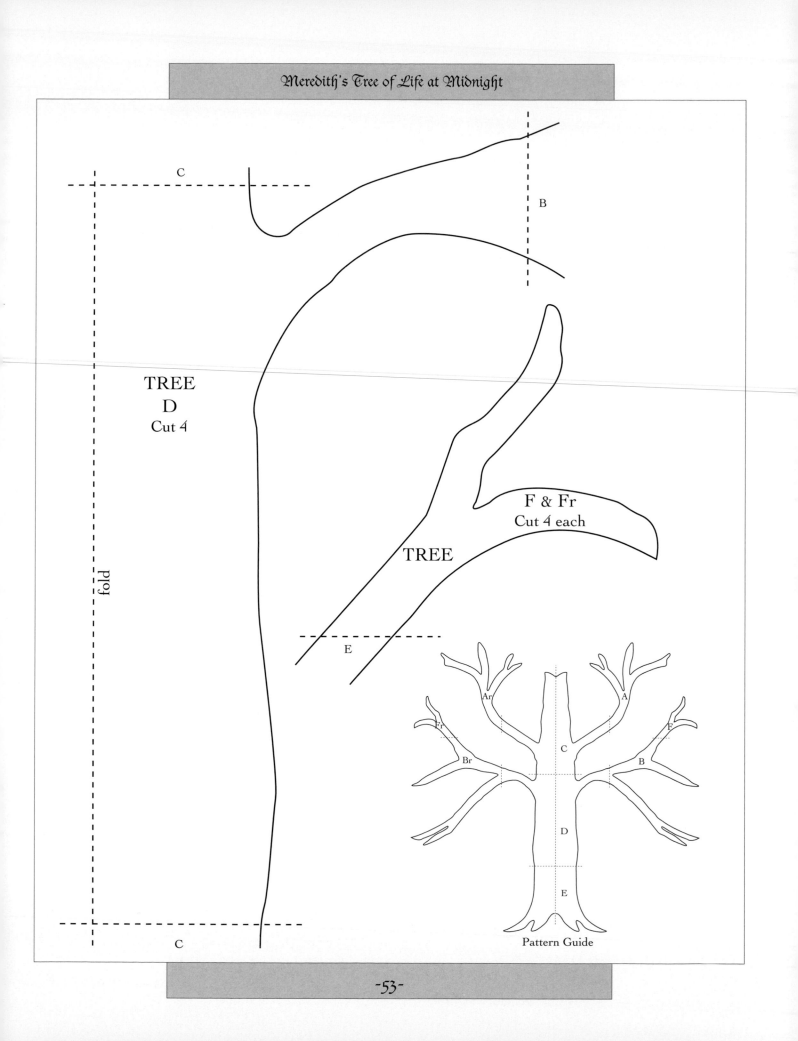

C

B

TREE
D
Cut 4

fold

F & Fr
Cut 4 each

TREE

E

Pattern Guide

C

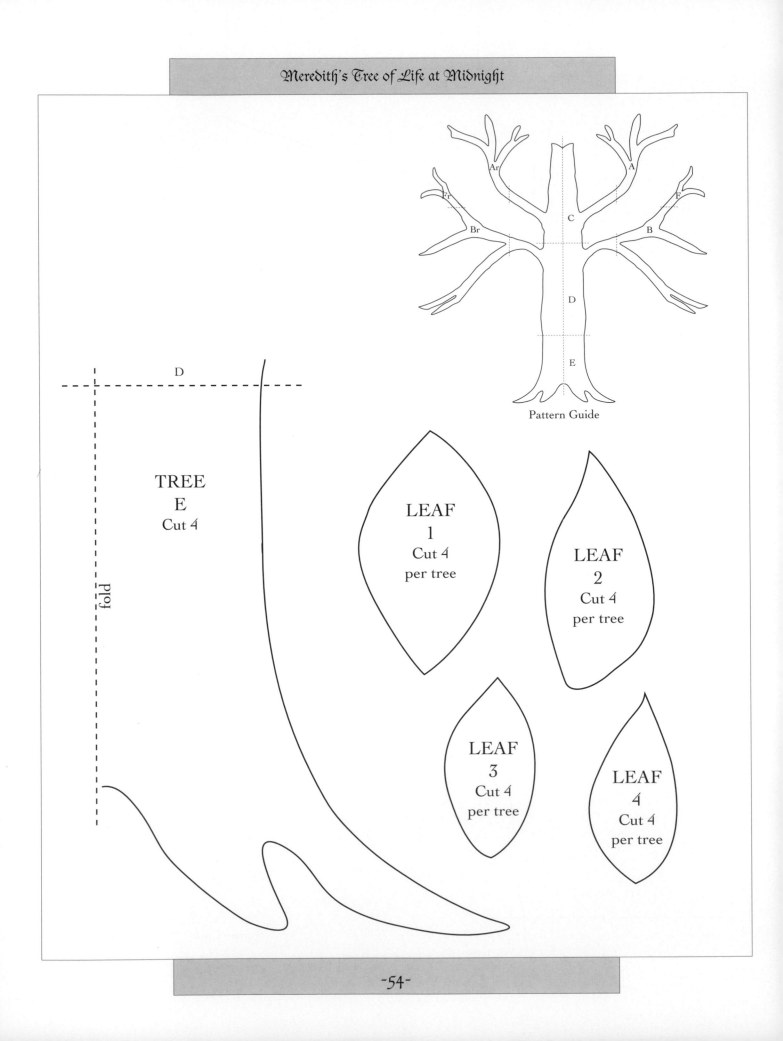

Pattern Guide

TREE
E
Cut 4

fold

D

LEAF
1
Cut 4
per tree

LEAF
2
Cut 4
per tree

LEAF
3
Cut 4
per tree

LEAF
4
Cut 4
per tree

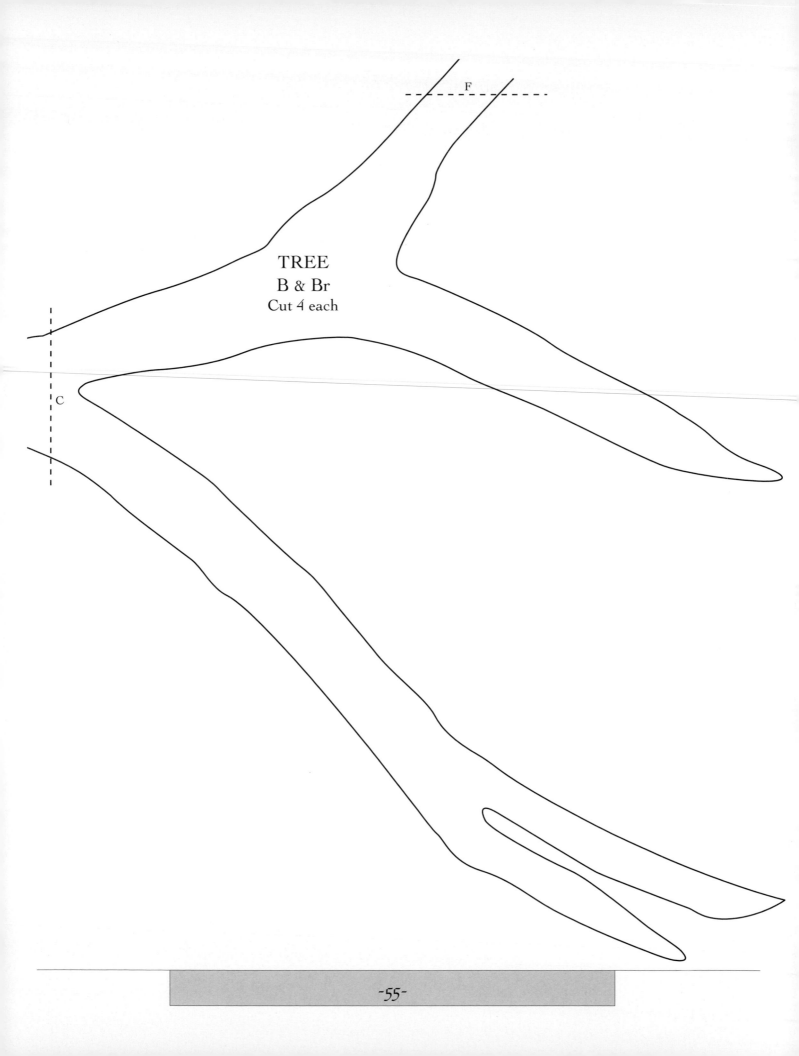

TREE
B & Br
Cut 4 each

F

C

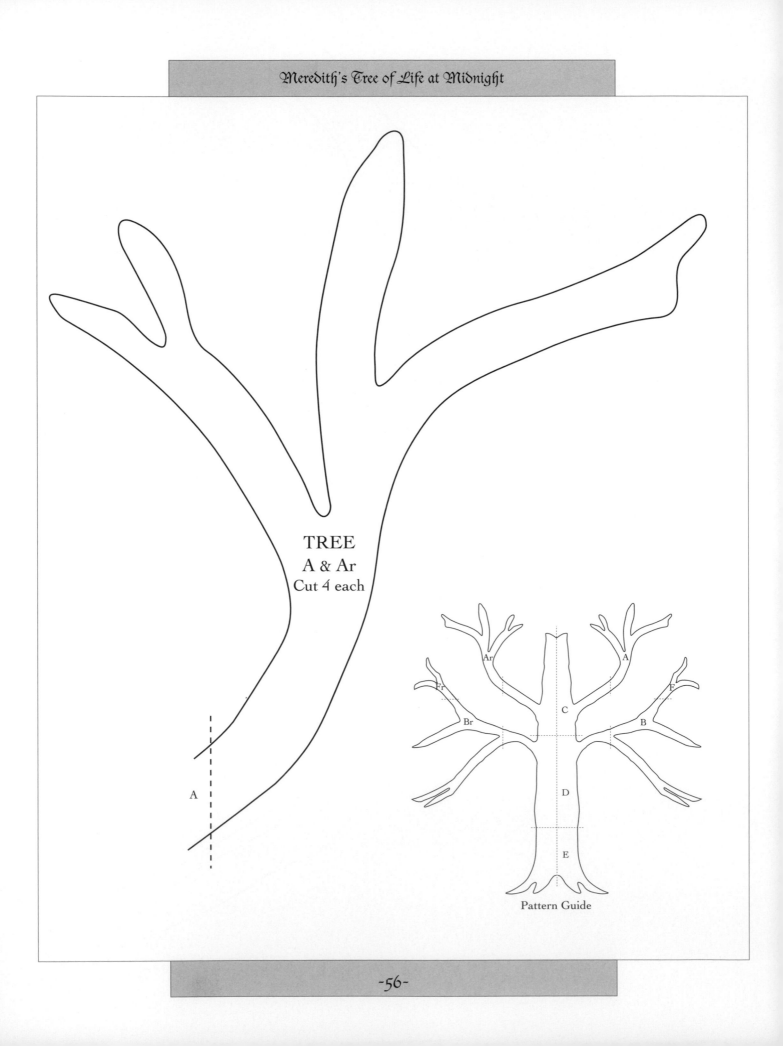

TREE
A & Ar
Cut 4 each

Pattern Guide

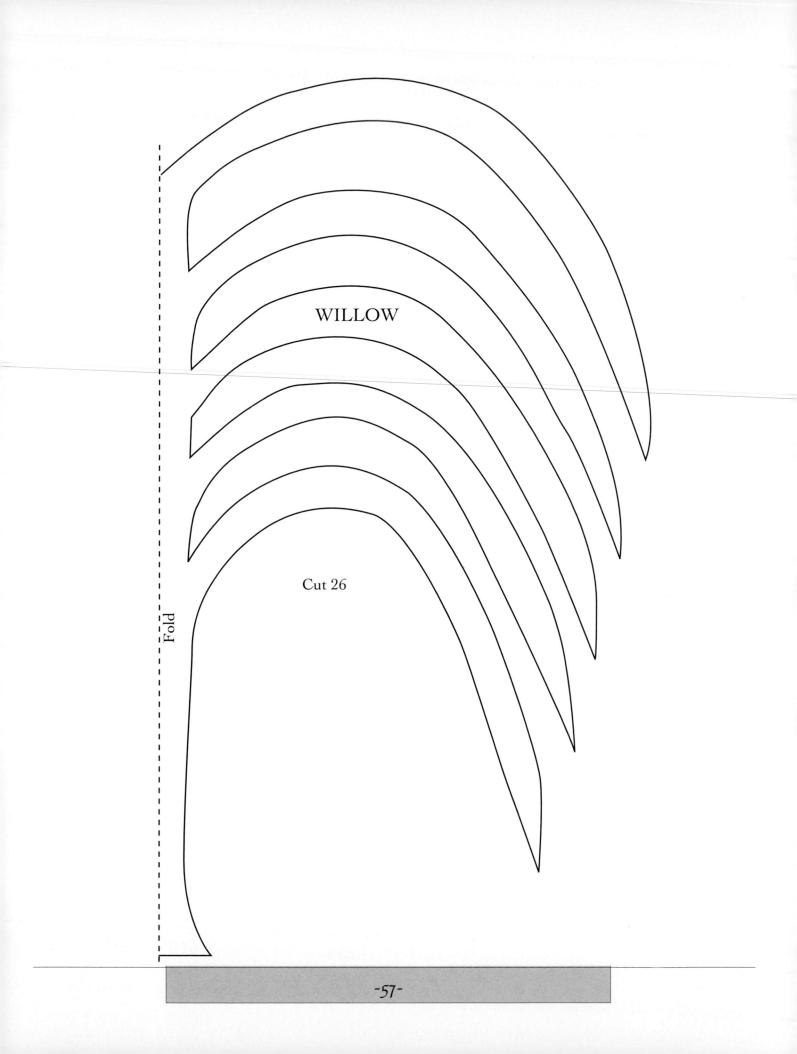

WILLOW

Cut 26

Fold

Add face and body details
with embroidery stitches.

1 deer

2 ducks

1 raccoon

1 mouse

1 squirrel

1 rabbit

1 mouse head

1 mouse body

1 owl

1 turtle

1 wolf

Place against tree trunk

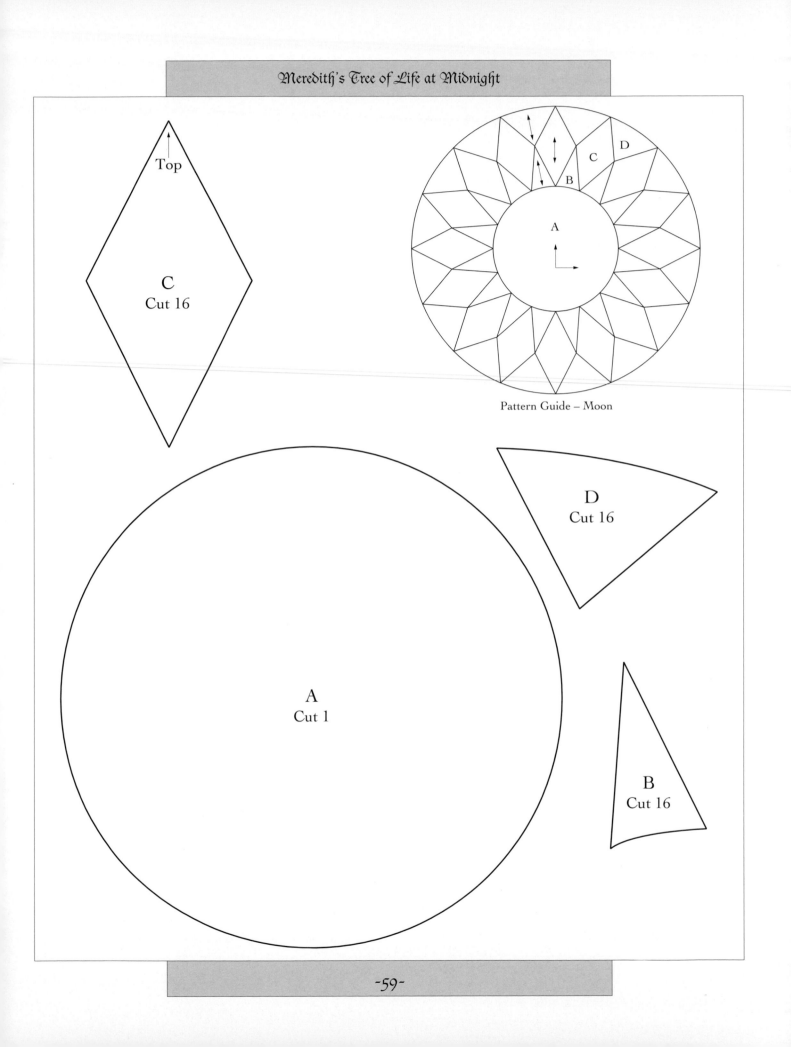

Top

C
Cut 16

Pattern Guide – Moon

D
Cut 16

A
Cut 1

B
Cut 16

COXCOMB CROSSING BLOCK
42" x 42" finished size

FABRIC REQUIREMENTS FOR 1 BLOCK
    1½ yd. white background fabric
    ½ yd. green
    ½ yd. red
    ½ yd. pink
    ½ yd. yellow

BASIC SEWING KIT
    2 large sheets template plastic
    Fabric scissors
    Template cutting scissors
    Piecing and appliqué needles
    Threads to match fabrics
    Fabric pencil

Cut fifteen templates as given. Trace around templates on wrong side of fabric. Add seam allowance to fabric pieces.

CUTTING INSTRUCTIONS FOR 1 BLOCK
- Cut (1) 42½" square of white for background
- Cut (1) piece A of yellow
- Cut (4) pieces B of red
- Cut (8) pieces C of green, cut (8) pieces C of pink
- Cut (8) pieces Cr of green, cut (8) pieces Cr of pink
- Cut (4) pieces D of green
- Cut (4) pieces E of green
- Cut (4) pieces F of yellow
- Cut (20) pieces G of pink
- Cut (16) pieces H of red
- Cut (20) pieces I of red
- Cut (4) pieces J of white, cut (4) pieces Jr of white
- Cut (4) pieces K of green, cut (4) pieces Kr of green
- Cut (4) pieces L of white, cut (4) pieces Lr of white
- Cut (4) pieces M of green, cut (4) pieces Mr of green
- Cut (4) pieces N of white, cut (4) pieces Nr of white
- Cut (4) pieces O of white

BLOCK ASSEMBLY (Patterns: pages 68–71)
- Sew crossing section of block. Piece Unit 1 by sewing a B to each side of A. Fig. 1.
- Make four Unit 2's by first piecing 16 sets of one green C and one pink C triangles to form individual rectangles. Repeat for Cr green and Cr pink triangles. Fig. 2.
- Sew two rectangles, short ends together. Keep C rectangles separate from Cr rectangles. Fig. 3.
- Sew stem D to a pair of C rectangles. Repeat with remaining three pairs of C rectangles. Fig. 4.
- Sew Cr rectangle pairs to other side of D stem units. Fig. 5.
- For top row of inner Crossing block, sew an O piece to each side of a Unit 2, noting the unit's direction. Fig. 6.

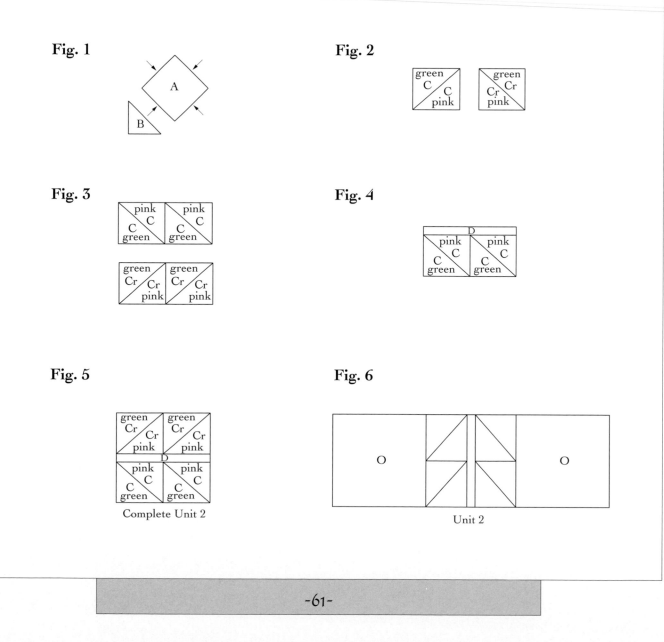

Fig. 1

Fig. 2

Fig. 3

Fig. 4

Fig. 5

Complete Unit 2

Fig. 6

Unit 2

- To complete middle row, sew two Unit 2's to each side of a Unit 1, noting opposing directions of the Unit 2's. Fig. 7.
- Sew the bottom row the same as the top row, but reverse the direction of Unit 2. Fig. 8.
- Join the top row to the middle row, abutting seam allowances of units. Then add to bottom row in same manner. Set aside this inner crossing section.
- To piece the Coxcomb sections, first separate fabric pieces and the reverse pieces. For the leaf section, Unit 3, sew J to K, then add L. Repeat for Jr, Kr, Lr. Continue in same manner for three remaining flowers. Fig. 9.
- Sew short stem E to J,K,L, then join the Jr, Kr, Lr section. Repeat for the other three flowers. Fig. 10.

Fig. 7

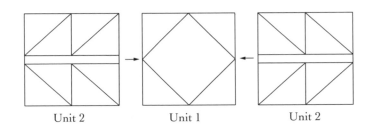

Unit 2   Unit 1   Unit 2

Fig. 8

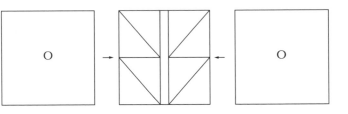

O   O

Fig. 9   **Fig. 10**

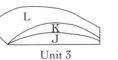

Unit 3

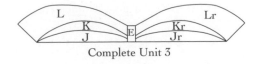

Complete Unit 3

- Piece F must be set into Unit 3 by first sewing the flat bottom to the top of E. Attach F's bias sides to L by starting at the corners of E and sewing towards the top arch of F. Fig. 11.

COXCOMB SECTION

- Sew five I's to five G's for each of the four flowers. (Hint: pin the beginning and end of pieces, then in the middle distributing fullness evenly. Clip only if necessary to ease curve.) Add H to one side of G-I section; then attach another G-I section to the H just sewn. Sew the two I's from their inner corners outward. Fig. 12.
- Continue adding H's to G-I sections on both sides of the center G-I section of the Coxcomb until the flower has four H's and five G-I's.
- Sew M to N. Repeat for Mr and Nr, and remaining three flowers.
- Attach M-N and Mr-Nr sections to the ends of the Coxcombs starting at bottom of first and last G's and sewing outward. Fig. 13.

Fig. 11

Fig. 12

Fig. 13

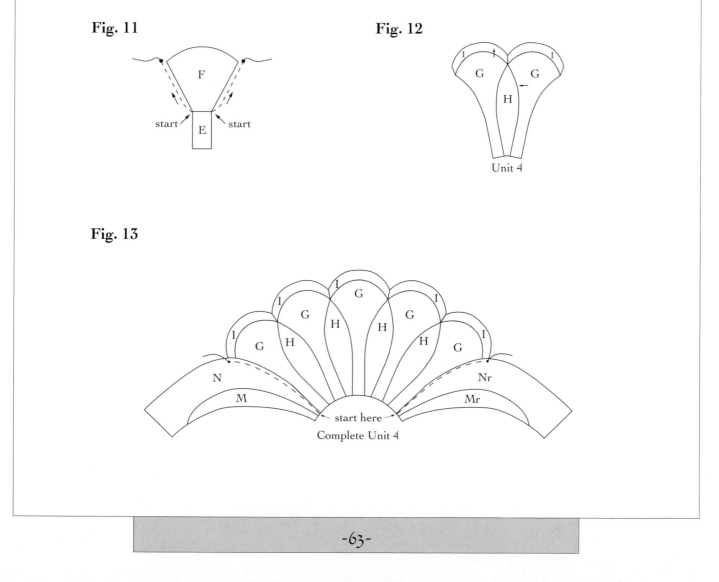

-63-

• Sew leaf, Unit 3, to Coxcomb, Unit 4. The yellow center F will be pinned and sewn first. Starting where the inner edge of Lr meets Mr, pin F piece of Unit 3 to Unit 4, ending with M being even with the curved edge of F. Ease, if necessary, and sew. Fig. 14a. Sew remaining parts of Units 3 and 4 by starting at outer corner of F, pinning L to M and sewing outward. Fig. 14b. Repeat at beginning corner of F for attaching Lr to Mr. Complete remaining flowers in the same manner.

Fig. 14 a & b

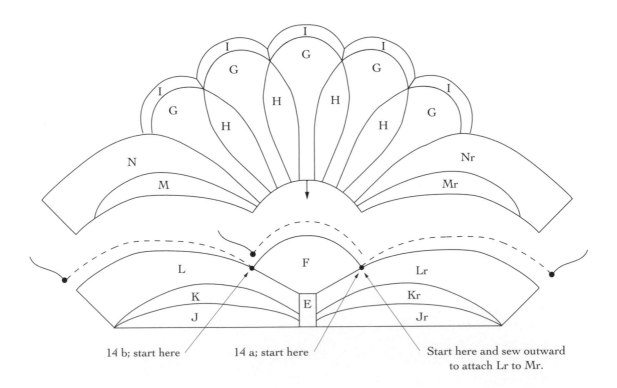

14 b; start here

14 a; start here

Start here and sew outward to attach Lr to Mr.

• Sew Coxcombs to Inner Crossing. Sew bottoms of Unit 3's to four sides of inner Crossing section. Attach diagonal edges of LMN to adjacent Coxcomb by starting at inner corner of block and sewing outward. Repeat for all corners, see page 66. Center and pin the block onto 42½" square background. Turn under on pencil lines of I, N, and Nr pieces and appliqué all edges down. Turn over and carefully cut back of block ¼"–½" away from appliqué stitching on back.

Coxcomb Crossing Corner

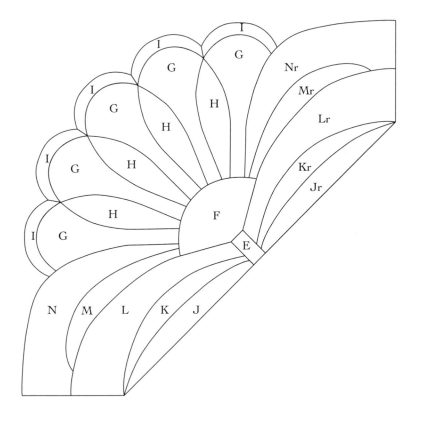

Inner Crossing Section

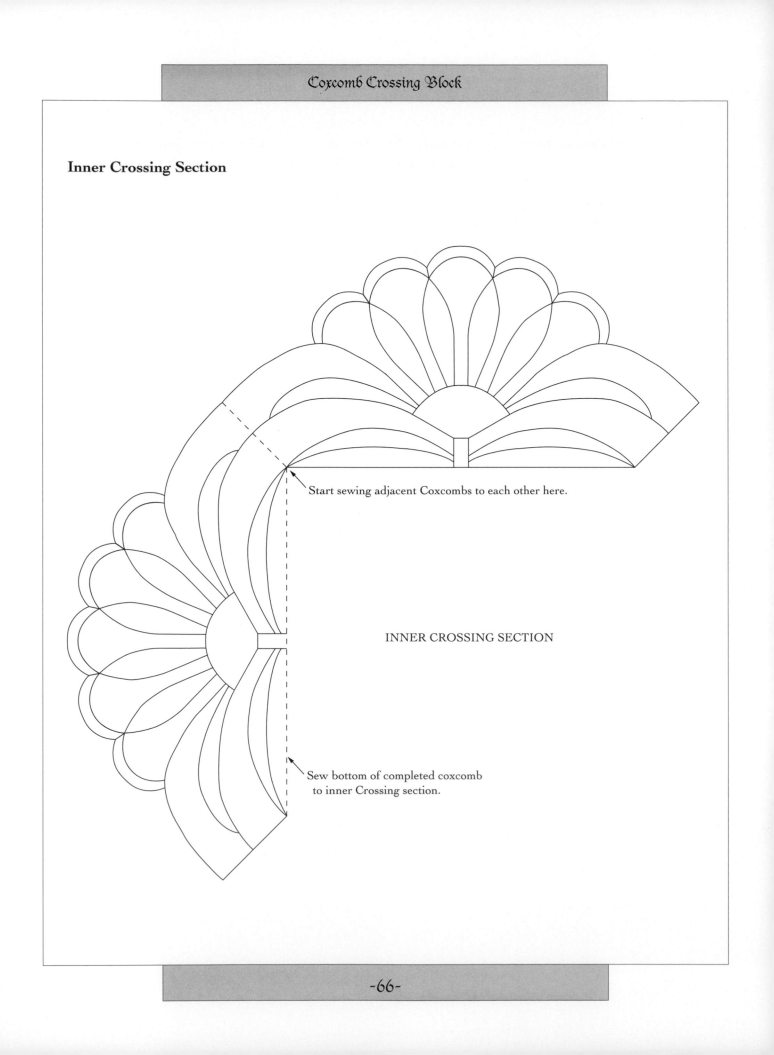

Start sewing adjacent Coxcombs to each other here.

INNER CROSSING SECTION

Sew bottom of completed coxcomb
to inner Crossing section.

Coxcomb Crossing Block

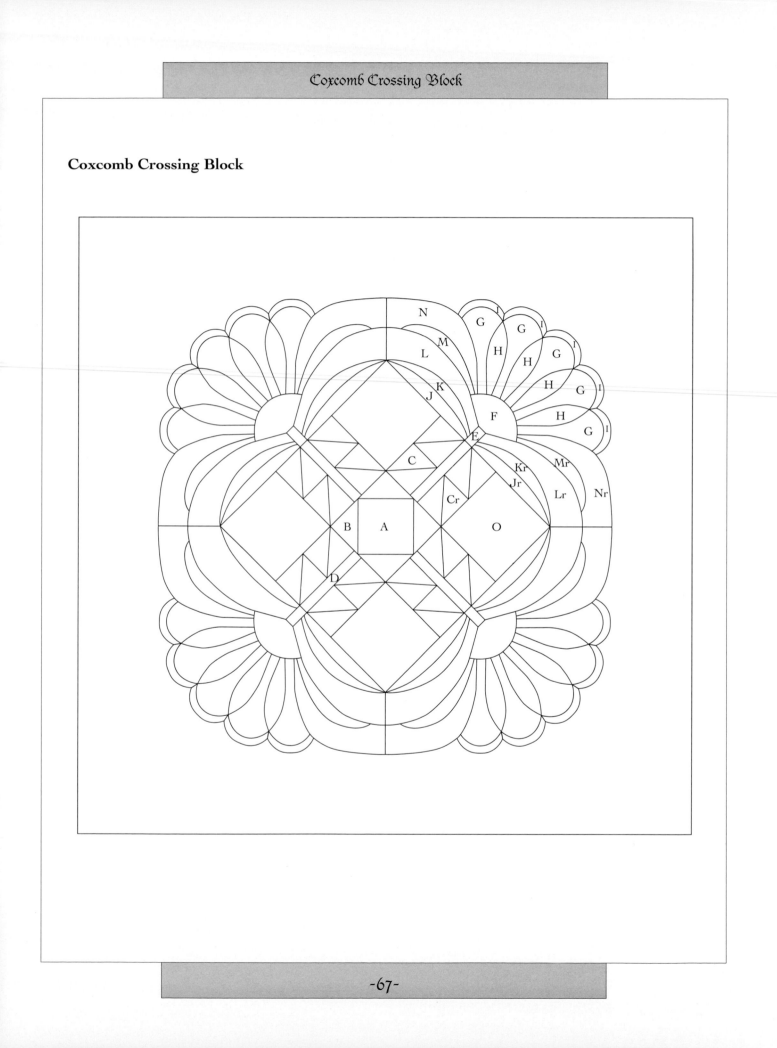

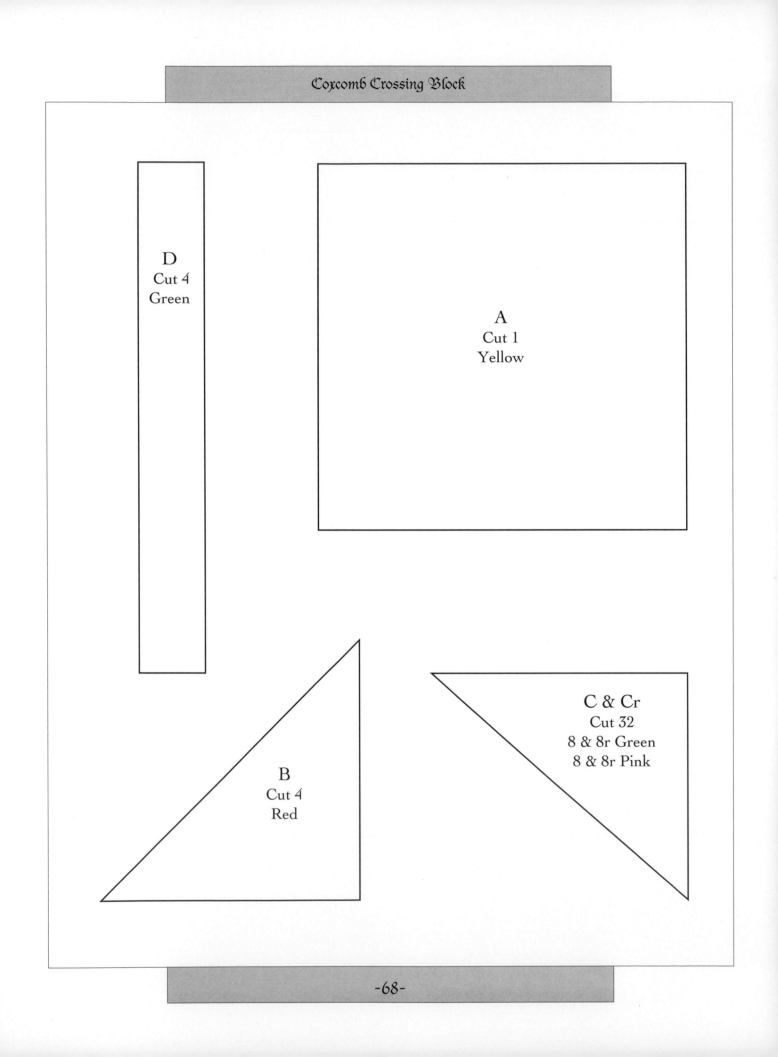

D
Cut 4
Green

A
Cut 1
Yellow

C & Cr
Cut 32
8 & 8r Green
8 & 8r Pink

B
Cut 4
Red

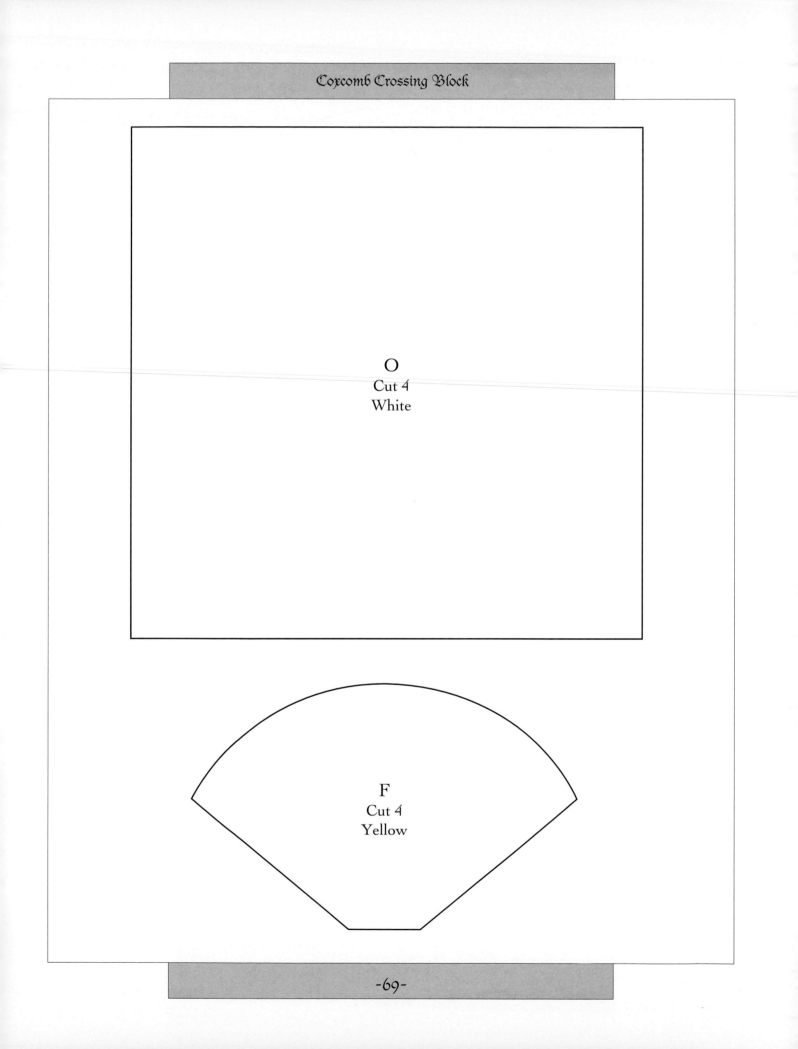

O
Cut 4
White

F
Cut 4
Yellow

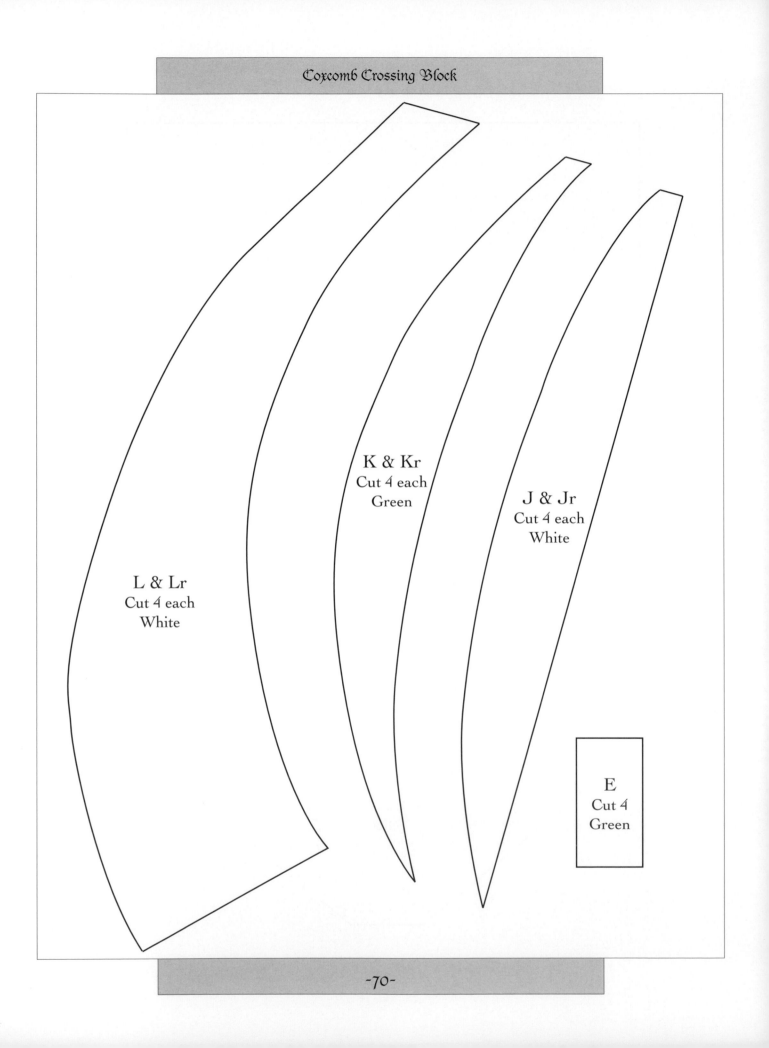

K & Kr
Cut 4 each
Green

J & Jr
Cut 4 each
White

L & Lr
Cut 4 each
White

E
Cut 4
Green

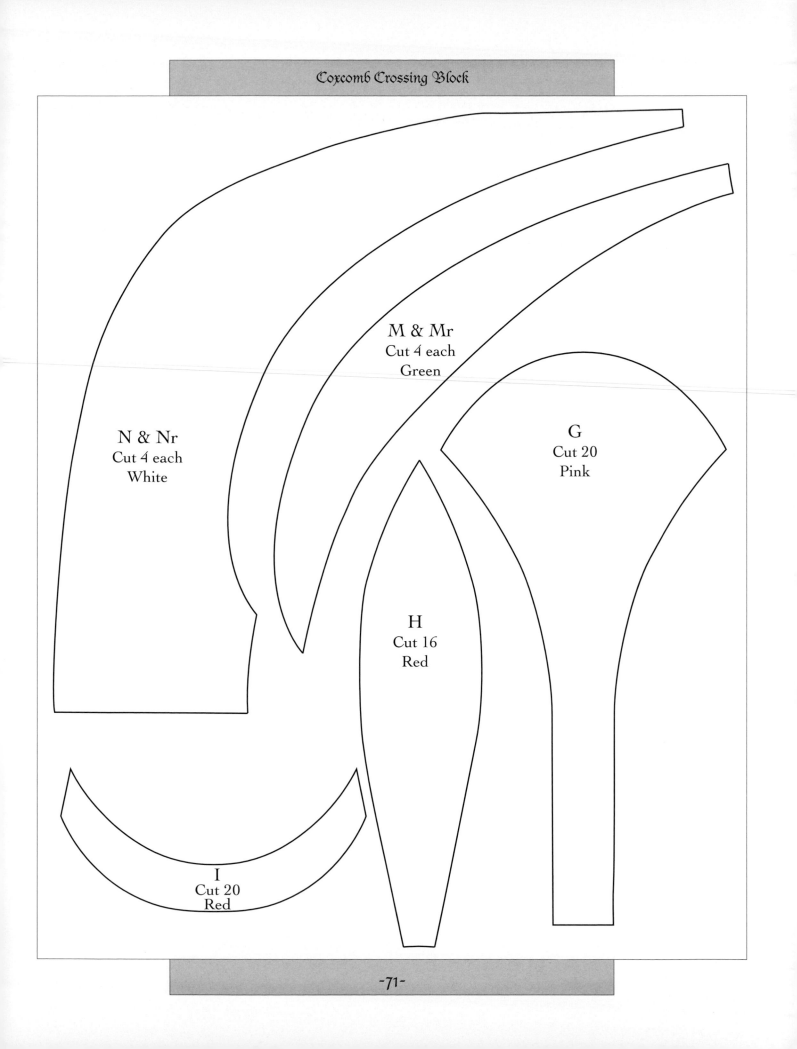

M & Mr
Cut 4 each
Green

N & Nr
Cut 4 each
White

G
Cut 20
Pink

H
Cut 16
Red

I
Cut 20
Red

WHIG-HARRISON ROSE
35" x 35" finished size

FABRIC REQUIREMENTS FOR 1 BLOCK
 35½" square block of background color
 12" square of yellow, center flower outer
  petals and four buds
 ¼ yd. red for five flower centers
 ¼ yd. dark red for center flower inner
  petals and flowers on rose branches
 ½ yd. dark green for branches and bud
  stems
 16" square medium green print for four
  leaves

BASIC SEWING KIT
 1 large sheet template plastic
 Fabric scissors
 Template cutting scissors
 Piecing and appliqué needles
 Threads to match fabrics
 Fabric pencil

CUTTING INSTRUCTIONS

Trace around all templates on right side of fabric, except Template B for the dark red flower petals. Trace B on wrong side of red since the short straight sides will be pieced.

BLOCK ASSEMBLY (Patterns: pages 74–76)

- Piece short straight sides of B's together to form a circle. Finger press under curved edges on pencil lines.
- Fold background block in half twice to find center. Finger press center and open.
- Position circle of B's in center and pin. Lay A over raw edges of B's inner circle. Needle turn under A's edges and appliqué.
- Finger press outer curved edge of C's on pencil line. Insert C's between B's and temporarily pin in place.
- Insert and position six-pointed leaves under Harrison Rose. Pin. Insert, position, and pin four E rose branches under Harrison Rose.

- Appliqué B's over C's, leaves, and rose branches.
- Appliqué C's down over leaves and rose branches.
- Finish sewing down leaves and branches, inserting four H buds where necessary.
- Position and appliqué red F's to G's. Position each F-G at the top ends of the rose branches and appliqué down.
- Option: number of bud stems can vary.
- Surround the Whig-Harrison Rose with a circle of buds. Trace the bud stem from the E rose branch onto top of dark green fabric. Using red, pink, and yellow, make buds using Template H on the right side of the fabrics. Only trace four yellow buds, which should be placed under the bud stems pointing towards the center Harrison Rose.
- Lay the bud stems around the floral "X" with the stems under the buds. Adjust so design is pleasing to the eye, and pin. Insert the buds, alternating the red and pink, and appliqué all pieces in place.

WHIG-HARRISON ROSE BLOCK

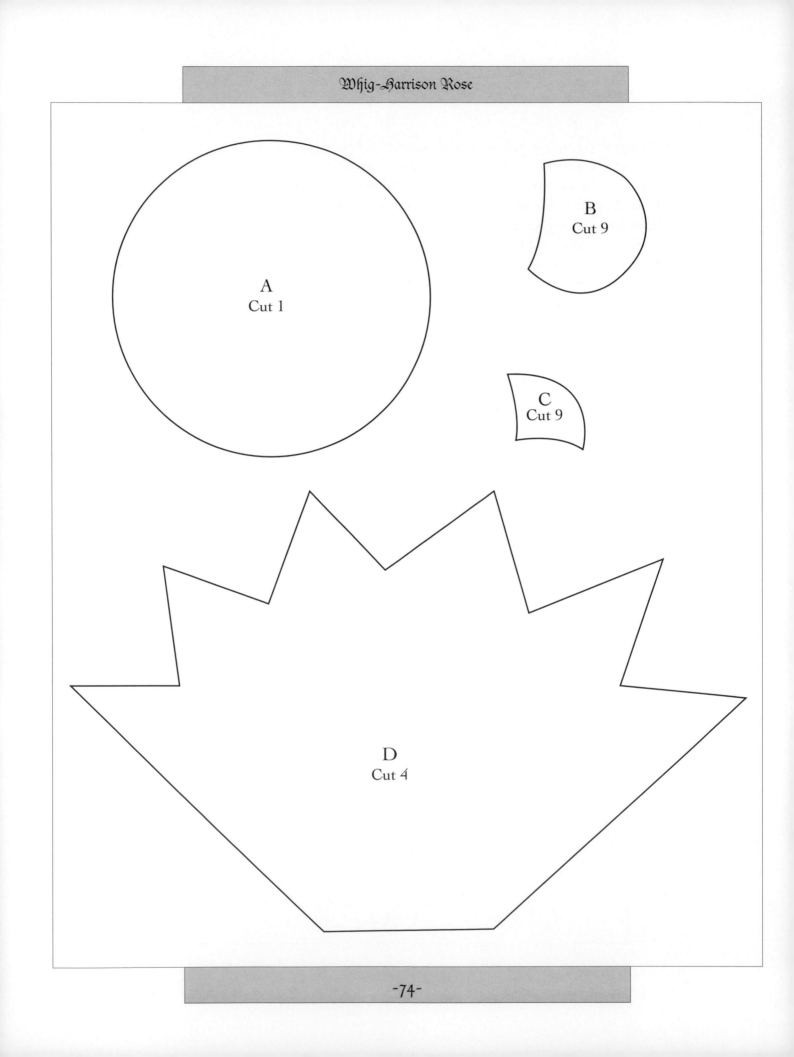

A
Cut 1

B
Cut 9

C
Cut 9

D
Cut 4

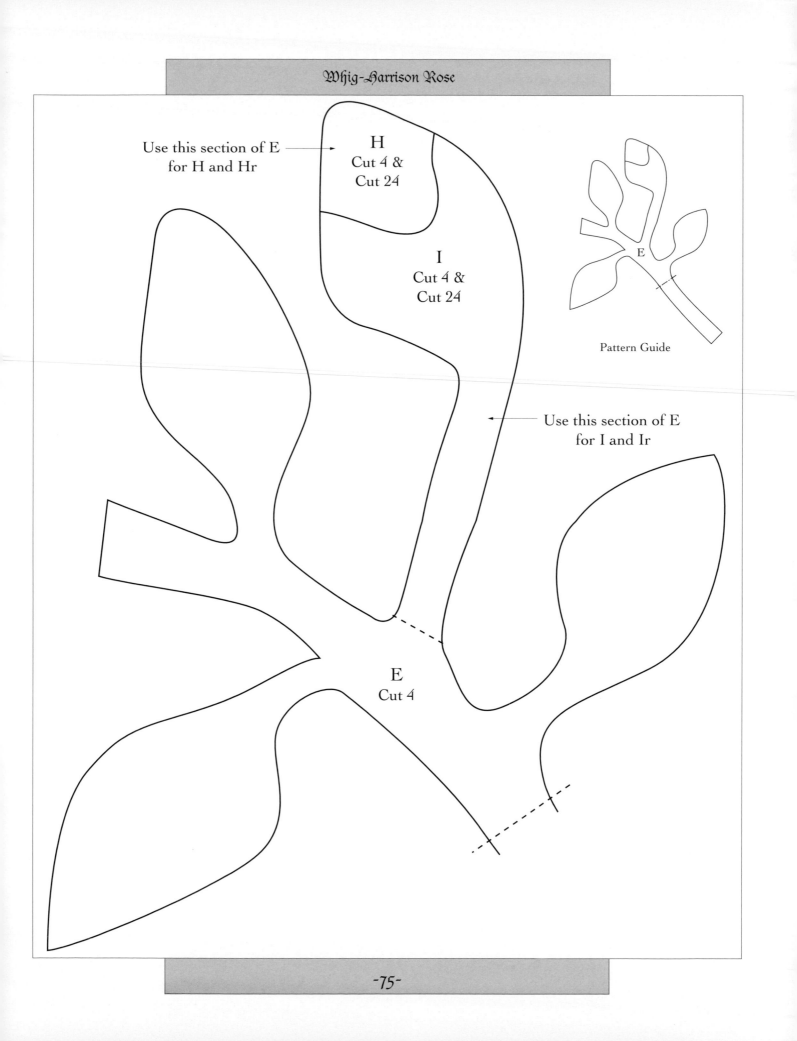

Use this section of E
for H and Hr

H
Cut 4 &
Cut 24

I
Cut 4 &
Cut 24

E

Pattern Guide

Use this section of E
for I and Ir

E
Cut 4

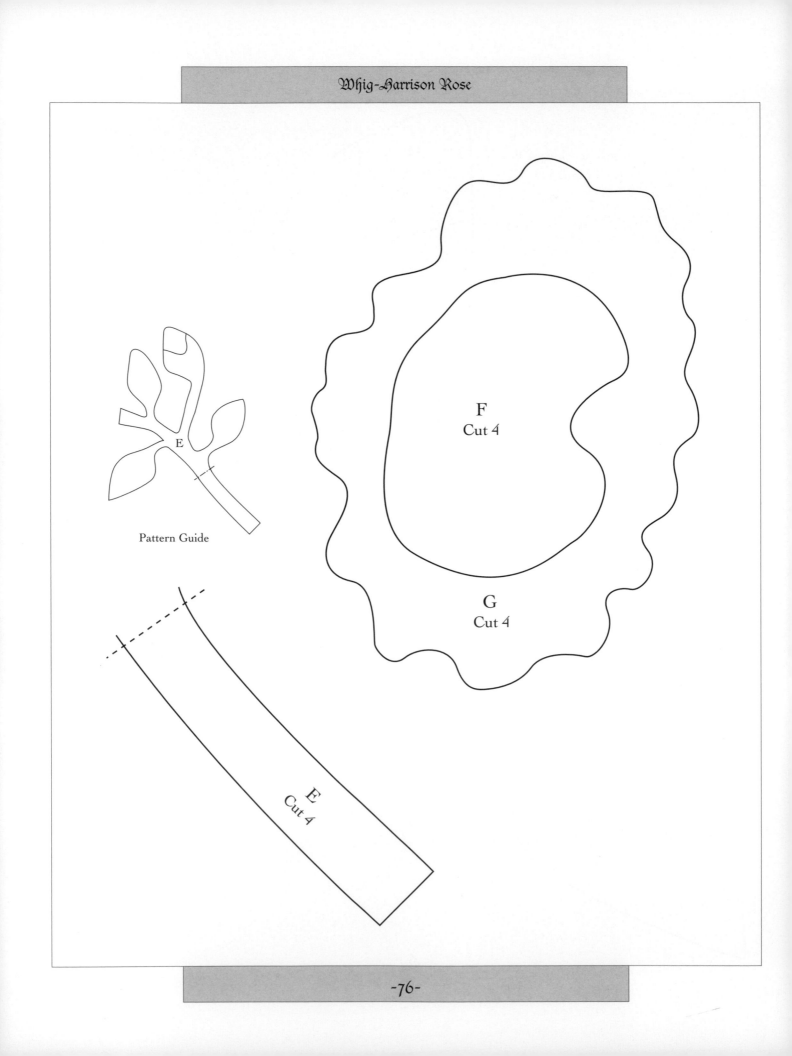

Pattern Guide

E

F
Cut 4

G
Cut 4

E
Cut 4

Princess Feather
102" x 102" finished size

Fabric Requirements

5 yds. for four (34½") blocks and reverse appliqué feathers in the border

5 yds. for four borders (two 17½" x 102½", two 17½" x 68½")

4 yds. for small accent stars, outer Dog tooth border, piping, and binding

3 yds. of one feather color, for feathers, large stars, and inner Dogtooth border

2 yds. of a second feather color, for feathers and medium stars

108" square backing for quilt

King size batt (cut to fit 108" square backing)

7¾ yds. of ¼" cording

Basic Sewing Kit

2 large sheet template plastic
Fabric scissors
Template cutting scissors
Appliqué needles
Threads to match fabrics
Fabric pencil

Make templates and trace around on right side of fabric for appliquéing. Add seam allowance to fabric pieces.

Cutting Instructions

- Cut (4) 34½" blocks of background color
- Cut (16) feathers of the first color
- Cut (16) feathers of the second color
- Cut (4) large stars of the first color (Add ½" turn under allowance when cutting out circle inside star instead of the usual ¼".)
- Cut (5) medium stars of the second color
- Cut (5) small stars of the third color

- Cut (2) borders 17½" x 102½"
- Cut (2) borders 17½" x 68½"
- Cut (4) 10" x 40" strips of background color for reverse appliqué in borders
- Cut (4) 2½" x 70" strips of first color for inner Dogtooth border
- Cut (4) 2½" x 103" strips of third color for outer Dogtooth border
- Make 11½ yds. of 1" bias from third color to cover cord for piping around outer edges of four sewn blocks

BLOCK ASSEMBLY (Patterns: pages 82–84)
- Instructions are for one block. Repeat process for remaining three blocks. Use needle turn appliqué technique.
- Find center of block by folding in half. Finger press. Fold in half again in opposite direction. Finger press. Open block and fold diagonally. Finger press. Repeat in opposite diagonal direction. Open block.
- Position large star in center with a tip pointing to the top of the block. Pin. (It will be appliquéd later.)
- Position and pin medium size star within the large star making sure a tip points directly to the top of the block, also.
- Turn under and pin seam allowance of large star center circle. (Clip were necessary.) Adjust this seam allowance so that when the medium size star is sewn, its points will just touch the edge of the circle.
- Clip inner points on straight edges of stars. See Fig. 1.
- Appliqué medium star in place. Position, pin, and appliqué small star onto medium star. (Option: appliqué the fifth small star onto the fifth medium star and set aside until all four blocks are joined together.)
- Starting halfway up the star side, turn under raw edge on pencil line. Appliqué on pencil line to star point. Take two stitches to hold it down. Needle turn the folded raw edge underneath the star point and back towards the sewn edge. Continue appliquéing down the other side of the star. When you come to the inner angle, take two stitches over the pencil line to anchor any frayed ends. Continue in same manner for rest of star. See Fig. 2.

Fig. 1

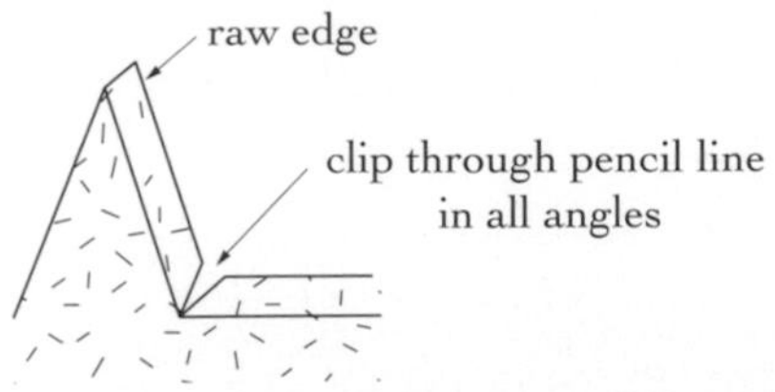

raw edge

clip through pencil line in all angles

Fig. 2

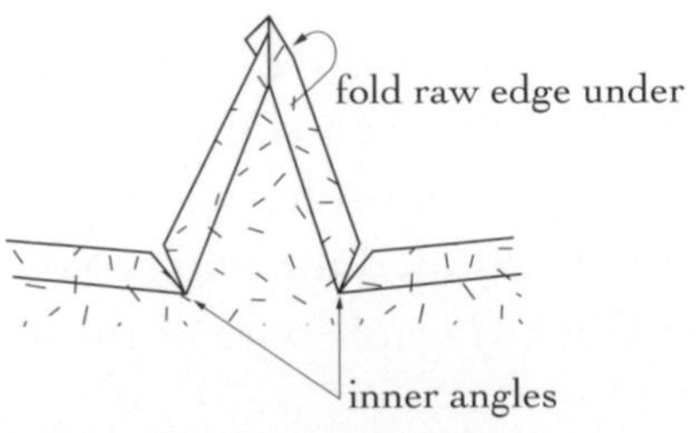

fold raw edge under

inner angles

- Using only 2–3 pins, temporarily position the eight alternating colored feathers between the large star points. Try to space them evenly, and carefully position their curvatures. Fold the spine's seam allowance under the star's inner angles. Pin.
- Appliqué the large star in place over the folded feather spines.
- Complete pinning of feathers. Needle turn feather edges so that marking lines do not show. Clip inner and outer curves where necessary cutting through the marked lines. This will ensure smooth feather edges as well as narrow spacing between the feathers.
- Join all four blocks when appliqué is complete.
- Position and sew down fifth appliquéd medium star at center juncture where all four blocks meet.

PIPING

- Fold 1" wide bias in half (wrong sides together)with one 70" cording tucked inside. Using zipper foot on sewing machine, sew ⅛" away from cording the length of the bias. See Fig. 3. Hint: lay cording a scant ¼" away from bias raw edge. This will prevent corner bunching. Continue in same manner for remaining three cords.
- Hand or machine sew piping to four blocks. Matching raw edges of piping to front side of joined blocks, stitch next to cording inside first stitching line. Trim any excess piping.

REVERSE APPLIQUÉ ON 17½" WIDE BORDERS

- Fold borders in half to find center. Finger press. Center medium size star template on fold 4½" from bottom of border. Trace.
- Trace around feather template with spines tucked under the middle east-west star points. (Reverse the template for the left side.) Using long stitches, baste the 10" x 40" background strips behind the tracing marks to the back of the border. (Right side of 10" x 40" strip to wrong side of border.) Carefully start trimming inside the tracing lines ¼" for the reverse appliqué seam allowance. Do not cut background strip underneath. Use thread to match border fabric. Clip inner and outer curves as necessary on feathers, as before. Reverse appliqué all four borders.

Fig. 3

Fig. 4

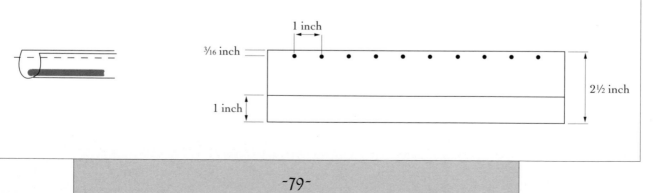

FIRST DOGTOOTH BORDER

- On each 2½" x 70" strip very lightly with a chalk pencil draw a dotted line 1" from raw edge the length of the strip. See Fig. 4 on page 79.
- On remaining long raw edge, mark a dot every 1" about ³⁄₁₆" from raw edge.
- Pin to a 17½" x 68½" border. See Fig. 5. Starting at right edge of border, fold under ¼" of Dogtooth border to hide its raw edge. Starting at first dot, cut a vertical line down to the 1" dotted chalk line. Cut every other dot, only a few at a time being careful only to cut the Dogtooth border.
- Start appliquéing at the folded edge of the Dogtooth border. Sew up to the point treating it the same as the star point. Before coming down the left side of the tooth, fold the triangular raw edge under so that it is about a 60° angle. See Fig. 6. Take two stitches to hold the inner angle securely before folding back the right side of the tooth to continue the process. Don't worry if you have a partial or whole dogtooth at the end of the border. When all four borders are sewn to the blocks, a separate Dogtooth can be appliquéd over the corners to make them turn correctly. (Our ancestors did this, and we can too!)

Fig. 5

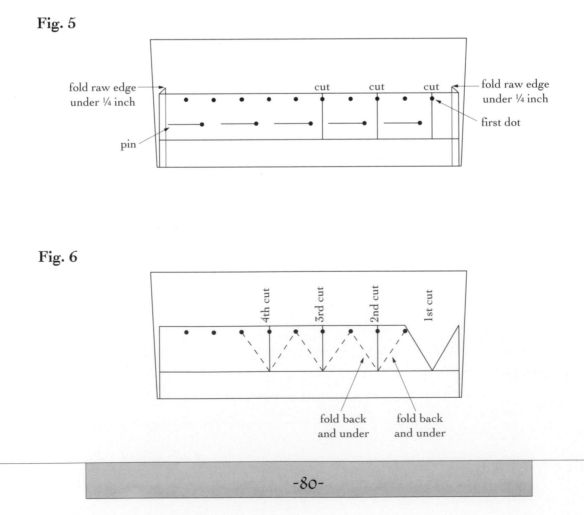

Fig. 6

- Turn border around so that the Dogtooth border points to the outer edge of the quilt when the border is sewn to the blocks. Sew border to blocks.
- Repeat steps for second 17½" x 68½" border.
- Lay quilt on floor or table to determine where to begin pinning the third 2½" x 70" Dogtooth inner border.
- Align 17½" x 102½" border with quilt top. Lay third inner Dogtooth border on top with right hand raw edge turned under ¼", pin in place. Repeat instructions for the fourth inner Dogtooth border.

SECOND DOGTOOTH BORDER

- Repeat instructions for Dogtooth border. The teeth will point to the inner border. Baste top, batting, and backing together after drawing quilting lines. Quilt as desired. Bind with 412" x 2½" bias binding. Fold in half and sew (wrong sides together) raw edges even with top of quilt sandwich. Miter corners, bring fold over to back, and appliqué down.

Full Quilt

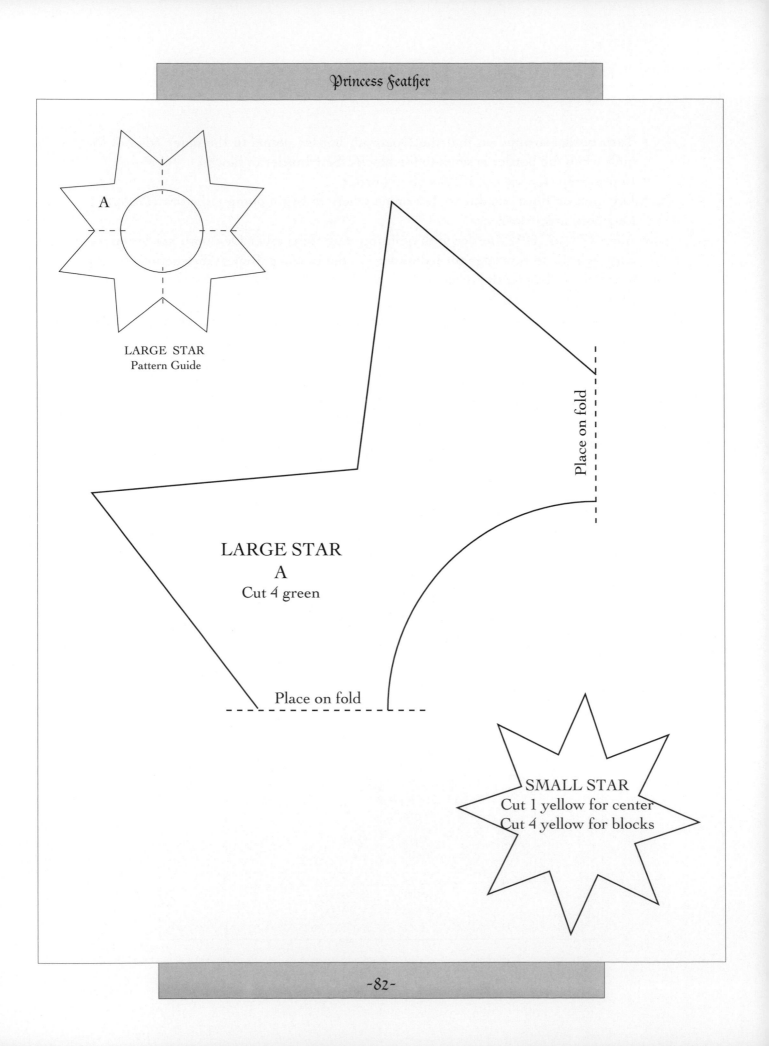

A

LARGE STAR
Pattern Guide

LARGE STAR
A
Cut 4 green

Place on fold

Place on fold

SMALL STAR
Cut 1 yellow for center
Cut 4 yellow for blocks

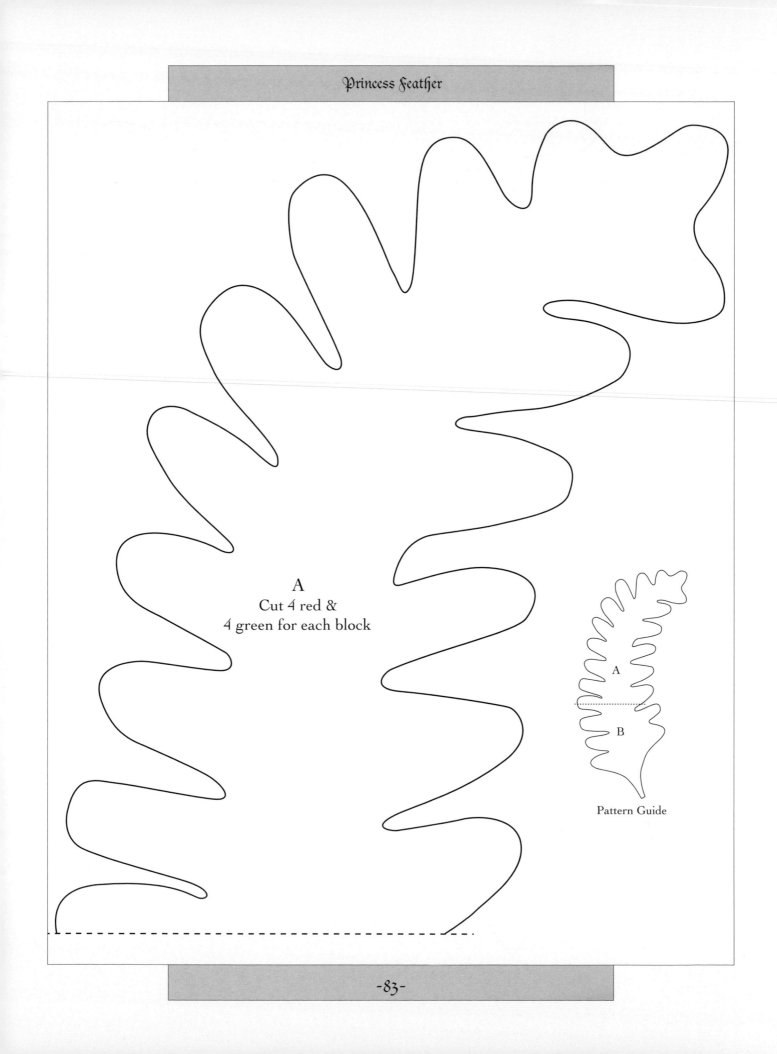

A
Cut 4 red &
4 green for each block

A

B

Pattern Guide

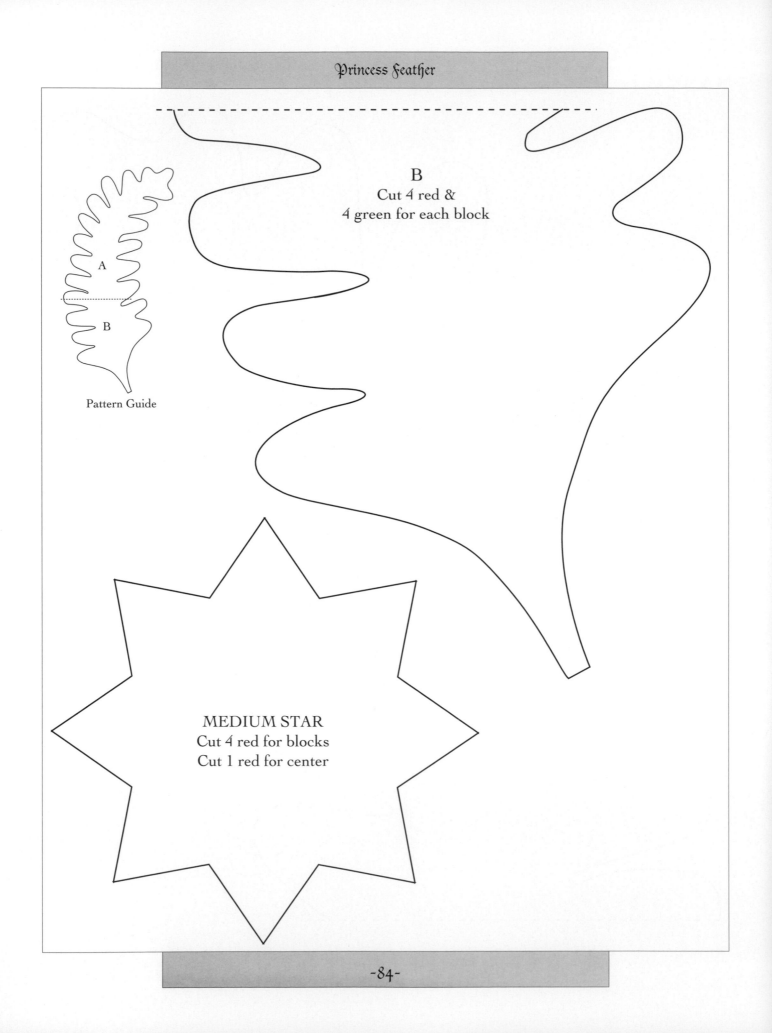

Pattern Guide

A

B

B
Cut 4 red &
4 green for each block

MEDIUM STAR
Cut 4 red for blocks
Cut 1 red for center

AMY'S WEDDING QUILT
90" x 96" finished size

FABRIC REQUIREMENTS
    8 yds. for four 36½" blocks, four borders:
        two 12½" x 72½", two 9½" x 96½" and
        binding
    ¼ yd. of main vase color
    ½ yd. of secondary vase color, and 1
        flower petal
    1 yd. for cherries and 1 flower petal color,
        center of heart
    ½ yd. for flower centers, top and bottom
        of vase
    2½ yds. green for leaves, stems, calyxes,
        border vine with bud branches
    Embroidery thread for cherry stems
    Batting and backing yardages to fit a
        90" x 96" top

BASIC SEWING KIT
    2 large sheets template plastic
    Fabric scissors
    Template cutting scissors
    Template pencil
    Piecing and appliqué needles
    Threads to match fabrics
    Fabric pencil

Make templates for pieced vase flowers, leaves, cherries, and vase parts. Remember to trace on the wrong side of the fabric for pieced flowers and vase. Trace templates on the right side of the fabric for individual leaves, cherries, vase top ring, vase handles, and vine bud branches. Make border leaf and bud branch templates. At times these templates will be reversed to fit within the borders. Add seam allowance after tracing onto fabric.

CUTTING INSTRUCTIONS
- Cut (4) A, (4) B, (4) Br, (4) D, (4) E main vase color
- Cut (8) C, (4) M, (4) Mr, (16) Q, (16) Qr secondary vase color and one petal color
- Cut (4) F, (4) V, (4) O, (16) P vase top and bottom color and flower centers

- Cut (64) G, (4) L, (4) Lr, (4) N, (4) Nr, (16) R, (16) Rr flower petals and cherries
- Cut (4) H, (4) Hr, (4) I, (40) J, (4) K (4) Kr, (16) S, (16) Sr (4) T, (4) Tr, (4) U, (4) Ur green stems, leaves, and calyxes.
- Cut border leaves and bud branches to fit undulating vine when concave and convex curves are determined.
- Cut two adult birds with wings from favorite scraps. Reverse one so they face each other. Make as many baby bird grandchildren as you desire!

BLOCK ASSEMBLY (Patterns: pages 91–102)
- Instructions are for one block. Repeat for other three blocks. See piecing diagram on page 90.
- Vase: piece short bottoms of C's to each side of D.
- Sew short bottom of A to top of first C.
- Sew short top of E to long bottom of second C.
- Sew F to bottom of E.
- Pin vase to block about 2½" up from bottom center. Pin handles under vase sides with top of handles even with top of A raw edge. Needle turn edges of handles and appliqué.
- Appliqué sides and bottom of vase. Do not sew top as yet. Option: Appliqué one of the adult birds under the side of the vase as if it were shy and peering around the corner. Appliqué the other standing in front of another vase.
- Piecing the vase flowers. Piece large center flower piece K to L, then L to M, M to N, then N to the right curved edge of O. Repeat for Kr to Lr, Lr to Mr, Mr to Nr, then Nr to the left side of O.
- Join the bottom halves of the flower by abutting the seam allowances of each color and having raw edges somewhat even. Pin marked lines at end of green calyx. Sew from bottom of O towards green calyx.
- Piece smaller flowers in same way sewing S to R, R to Q, and Q to the right side of P. Piece Sr to Rr, Rr to Qr, and Qr to the left side of P. Join the bottom halves of the small flowers in the same way as previous flowers.

ATTACHING THE VASE RING AND POSITIONING THE FLOWERS See page 90.
- Position the vase ring around the top of the vase. Tuck in H and Hr cherry branches about ¾" above vase handles. Appliqué the outside edge of the vase ring folding under and catching cherry branch raw edges. Finish sewing down cherry branches. Position and pin center stem I, stems U and Ur, and stems T and Tr. Fold under raw edges and tuck seam ends under front of vase top ring. Stems should lay over the back of the vase ring. Needle turn under edges of stems and appliqué in place. Either leave ¼" openings to tuck in leaf points, or plan to appliqué leaves with their ends just touching the stems.

- Finger press under on the pieced flower edge pencil lines. Position and appliqué in place.
- Appliqué two leaves to each stem.
- Position and appliqué eight cherries around the cherry branches. Chain stitch cherry stems from the branches to the cherries.
- When all the blocks are done, stitch them together to form a square 72½".
- Center heart motif, courtesy of Elly Sienkiewicz and C&T Publishing. Trace heart and dove pattern onto heavy paper or plastic. Tape to a glass table or make-shift light table. Center quilt top over the design and turn on light. If the lines are not dark enough to see, re-trace the design. Using a light touch and light lead pencil, carefully trace the design onto the quilt top.
- Baste a 16" square of fabric used for cherries behind the heart and dove motif to the back of the quilt top.
- Beginning with doves, carefully snip away top fabric only, a scant ¼" away from the drawn line. This is the turn under allowance. Using thread to match the top fabric, reverse appliqué the raw edges to reveal the doves.
- Starting at bottom of heart, carefully snip away top fabric inside feathers to about ⅛" from the drawn line. Only cut a couple at a time since pinning the resulting narrow bias feather edges is tedious. Needle turn under the ⅛" seam allowance on the pencil line and reverse appliqué down.

BORDERS

- Trace undulating vine for 12" wide border lightly onto right side of fabric border 12½" x 72½". Spread out on table or floor. Lay 9½" x 96½" border forming a right angle on the left end of the drawn border. See Fig. 1.
- Lightly mark where the two borders meet at the inner corner. On the opposite side 1¾" from outside raw edge, mark a dot. This is where you start tracing the undulating vine for the 9½" x 96½" border.

Fig. 1

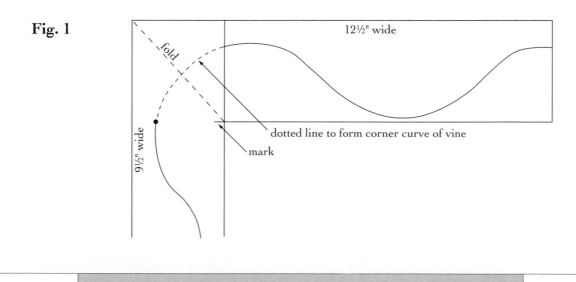

12½" wide

fold

9½" wide

dotted line to form corner curve of vine

mark

- Before tracing the vine for the longer side border, make a diagonal fold from the mark where the two borders meet on the inside corner to the outside corner. See Fig. 1. Finger press. This will help you visualize the highest point of the corner curve of the vine. Lightly draw a dotted line connecting the two vines in the corner curve. Repeat instructions for the remaining borders.
- Appliqué for borders. Make continuous bias strips to finish at 2¼" in width. A total of about 450" will be needed to accommodate the large curves in the vine.
- Fold and iron bias in half, wrong sides together. Position the raw edges a scant ¼" over the drawn line on the border. Pin several inches and sew down about ⅛" below drawn line. Use small stitches as this will be finished when it is folded up and over the raw bias edges and appliquéd down. See Fig. 2.
- Position border leaves and bud branches within the convex and concave curves now if you want to catch their stems as you sew the vine. Otherwise, plan to abut stems next to the vine after it is sewn. Remember to reverse leaf and bud branch templates to accommodate curves.
- Appliqué and reverse appliqué buds as needed. Appliqué as many baby bird grandchildren as you hope to have in the corners and on the vines.

FINISHING THE QUILT
- Sew borders to quilt, top and bottom first, then sides.
- Baste top, batting, and backing after drawing quilting lines.
- Quilt as desired.
- Bind with about 380" of 2½" wide continuous bias binding. With wrong sides together, fold in half making raw edges even with top of quilt sandwich. Miter corners, bring fold over to back and sew down.

Fig. 2

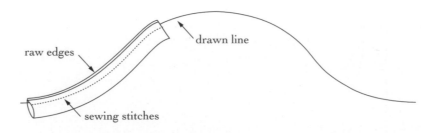

Full Quilt Diagram

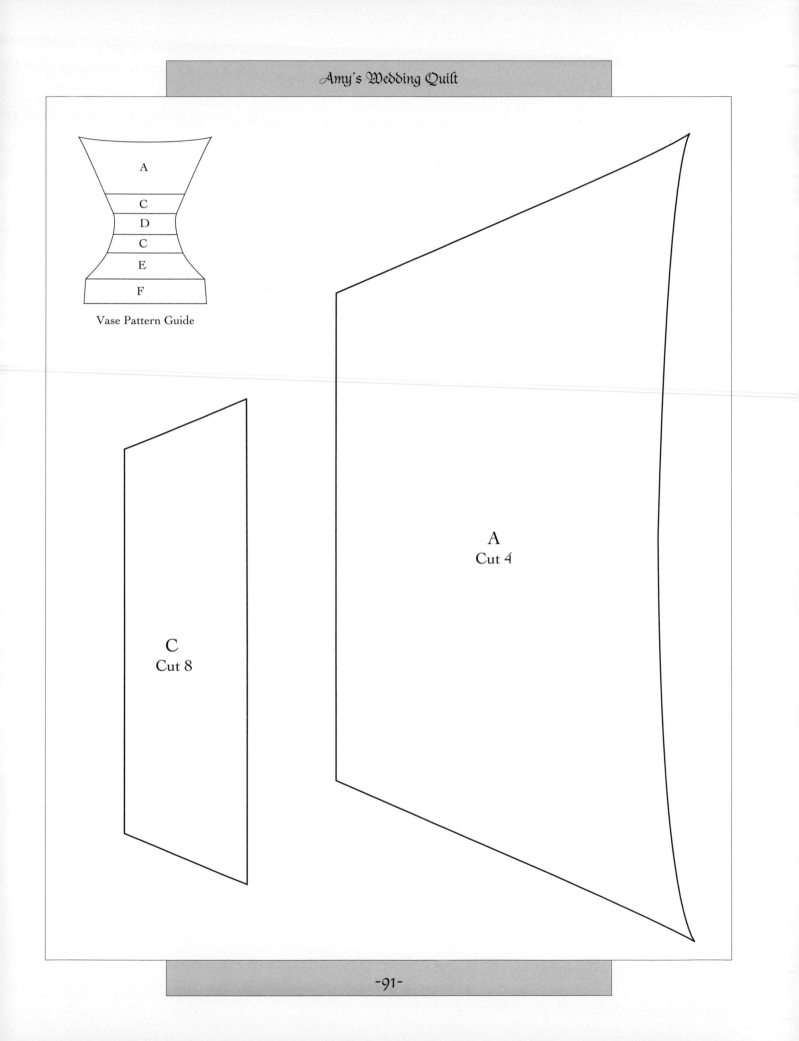

A

C
D
C
E
F

Vase Pattern Guide

A
Cut 4

C
Cut 8

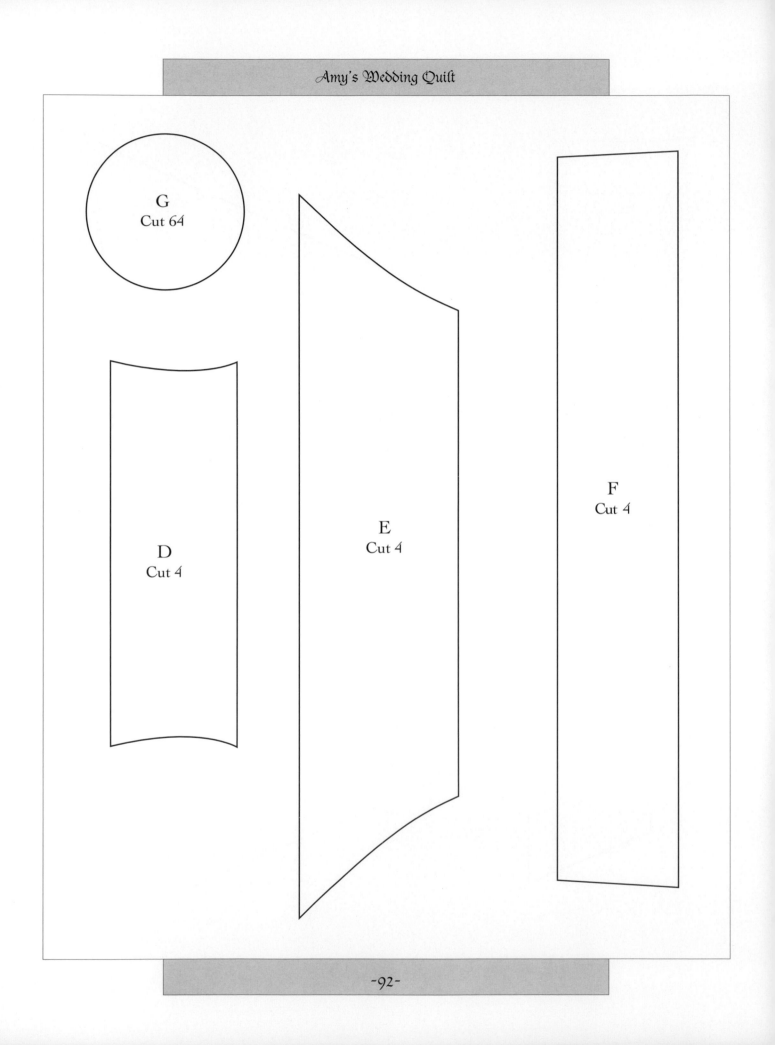

G
Cut 64

D
Cut 4

E
Cut 4

F
Cut 4

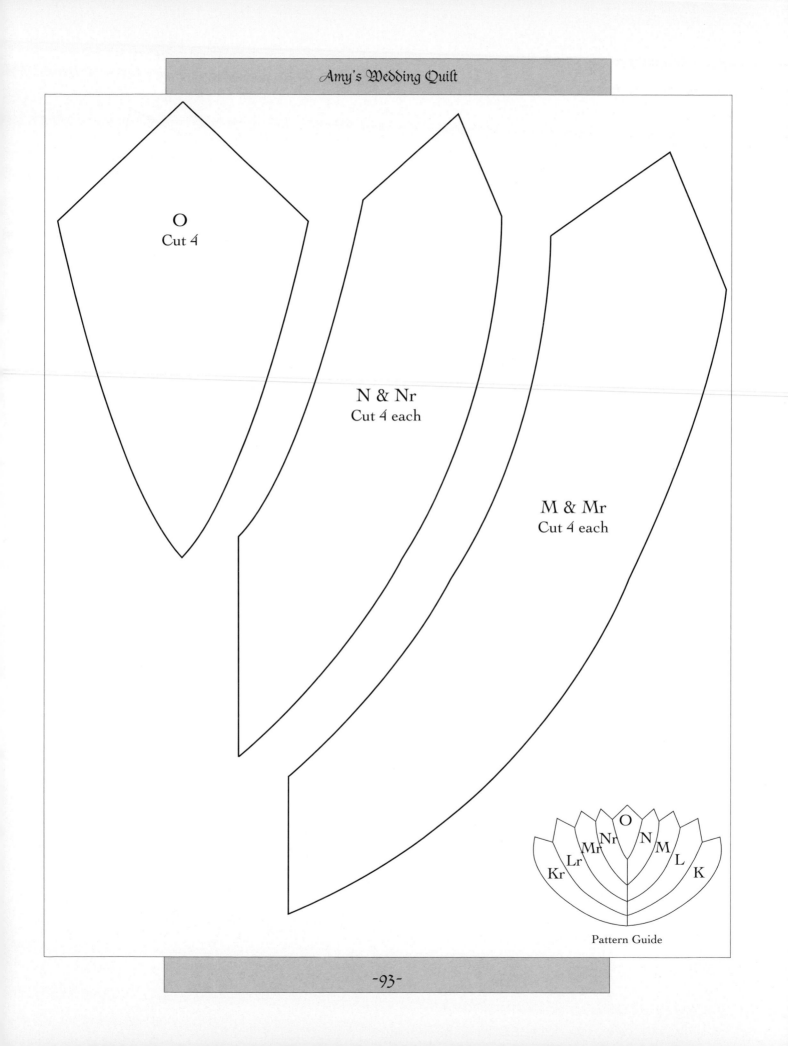

O
Cut 4

N & Nr
Cut 4 each

M & Mr
Cut 4 each

Pattern Guide

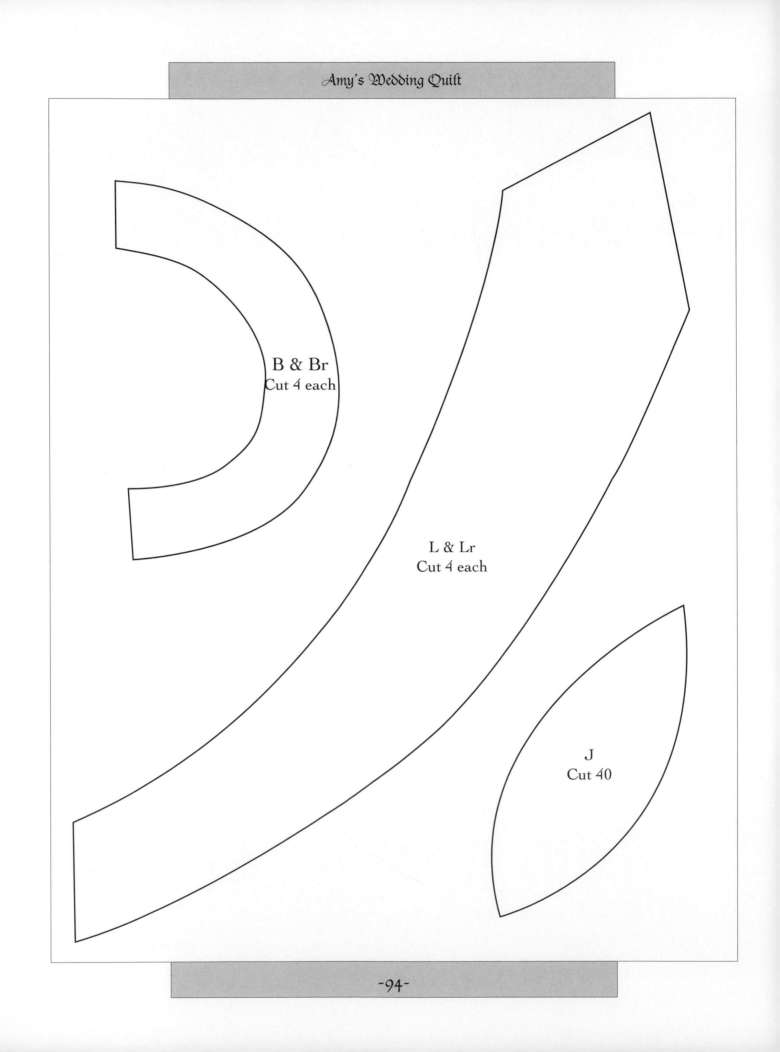

B & Br
Cut 4 each

L & Lr
Cut 4 each

J
Cut 40

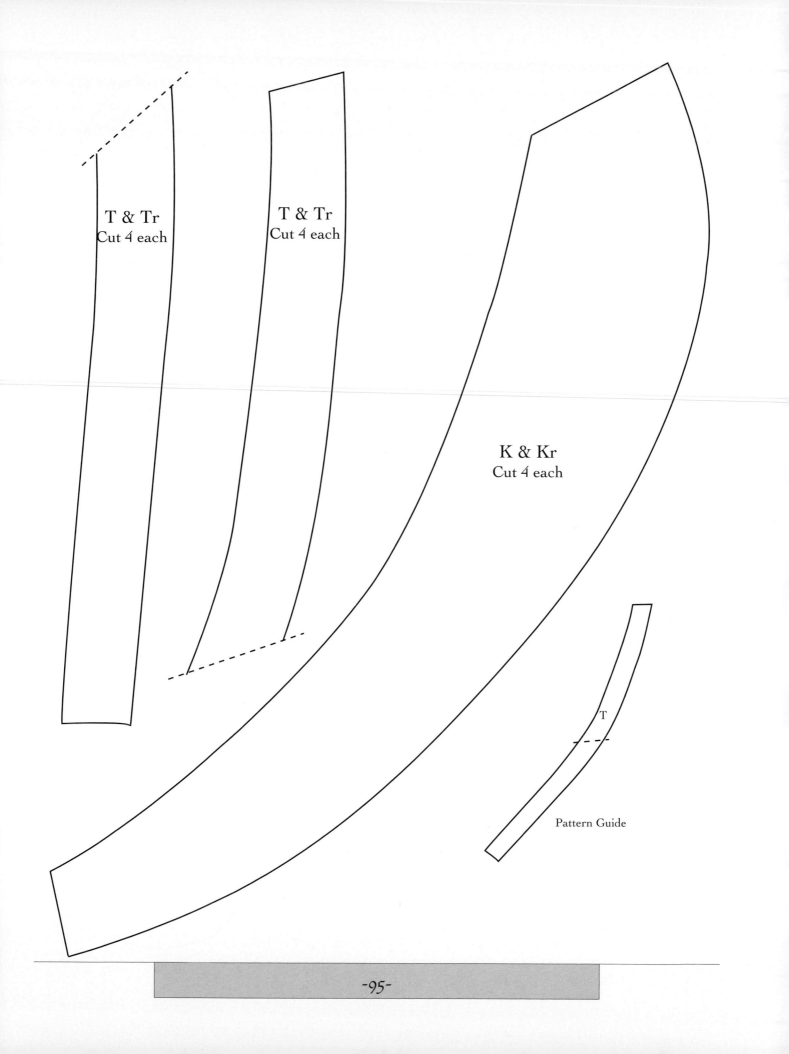

T & Tr
Cut 4 each

T & Tr
Cut 4 each

K & Kr
Cut 4 each

T

Pattern Guide

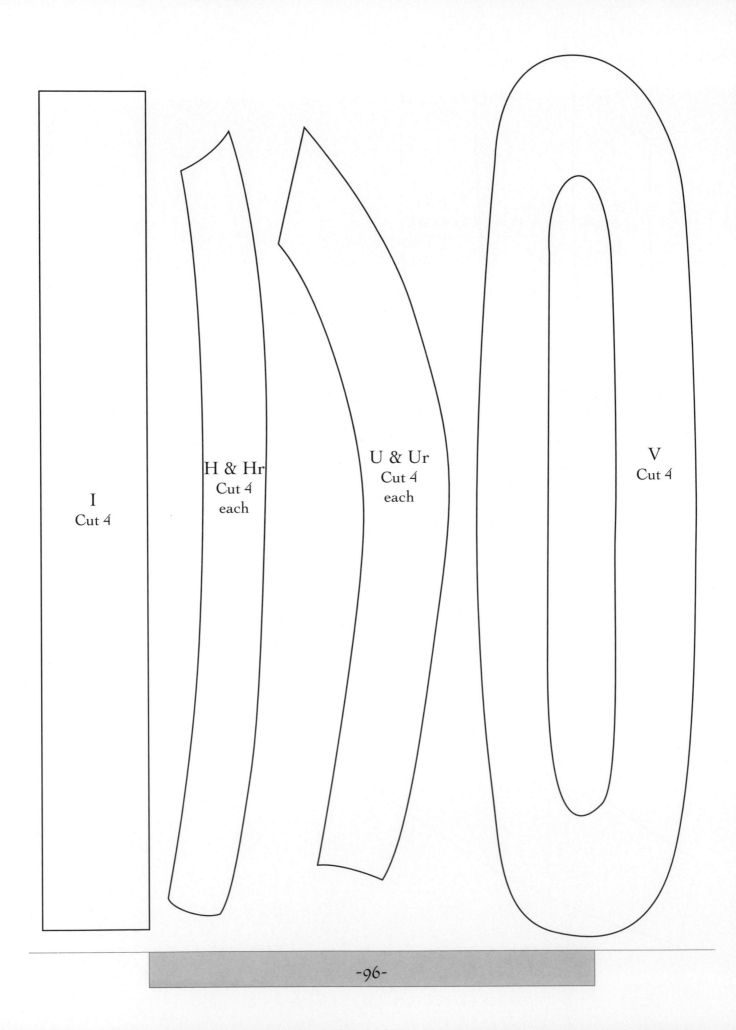

I
Cut 4

H & Hr
Cut 4
each

U & Ur
Cut 4
each

V
Cut 4

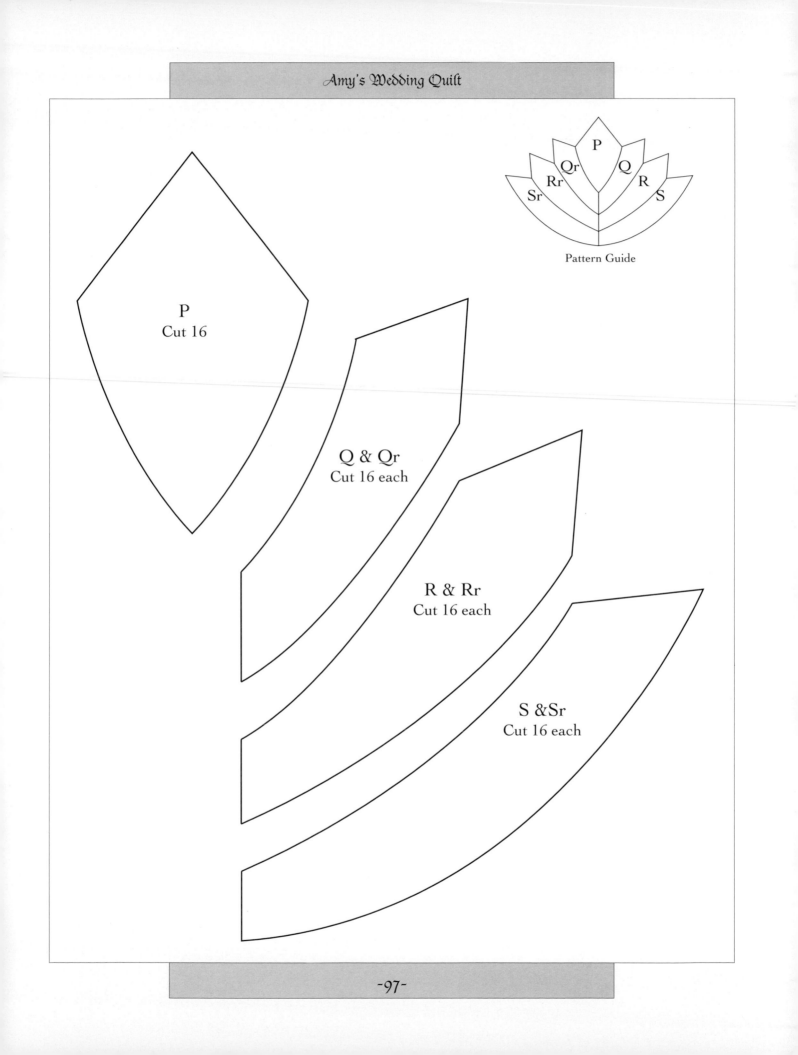

Pattern Guide

P
Cut 16

Q & Qr
Cut 16 each

R & Rr
Cut 16 each

S & Sr
Cut 16 each

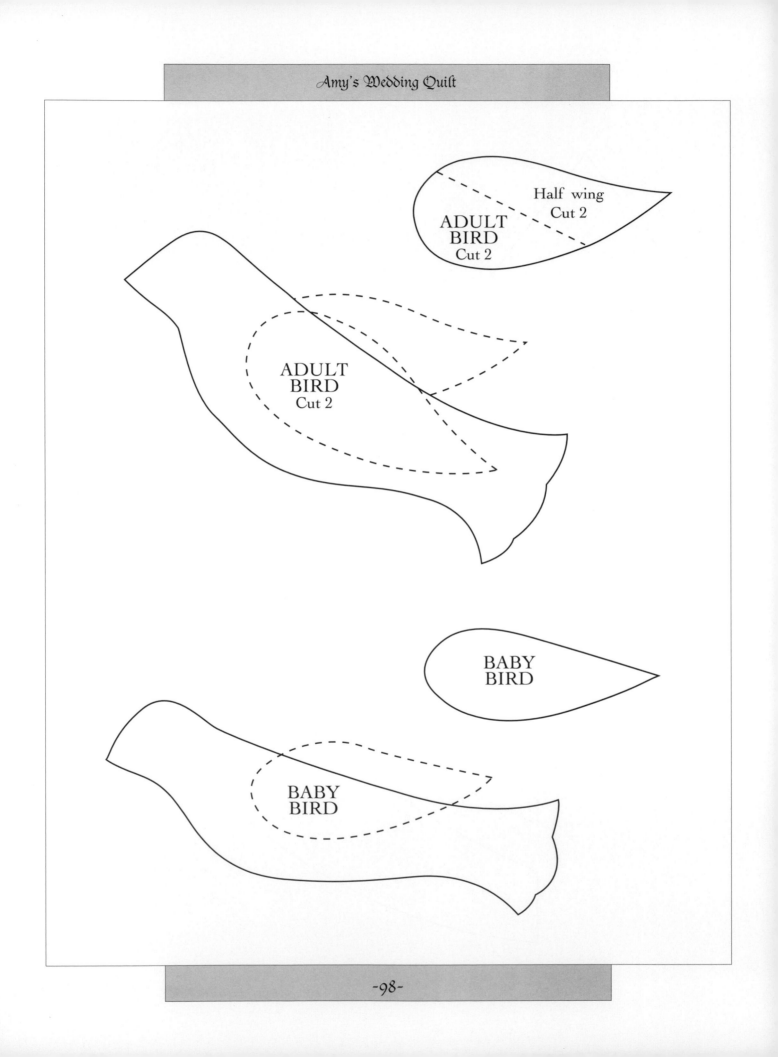

ADULT BIRD
Cut 2

Half wing
Cut 2

ADULT
BIRD
Cut 2

BABY
BIRD

BABY
BIRD

Quilting Design Guide

This original design by Elly Sienkiewicz is one of 24 patterns in her *Baltimore Beauties and Beyond, Studies in Classic Baltimore Album Quilts, Volume 1* (C&T Publishing, 1989). It is reprinted here with her permission.

"Feather-Wreathed Heart
with Doves"
Quilting Design

"Feather-Wreathed Heart
with Doves"
Quilting Design

This original design by Elly Sienkiewicz is one of 24 patterns in
her *Baltimore Beauties and Beyond, Studies in Classic Baltimore
Album Quilts, Volume 1* (C&T Publishing, 1989). It is reprinted
here with her permission.

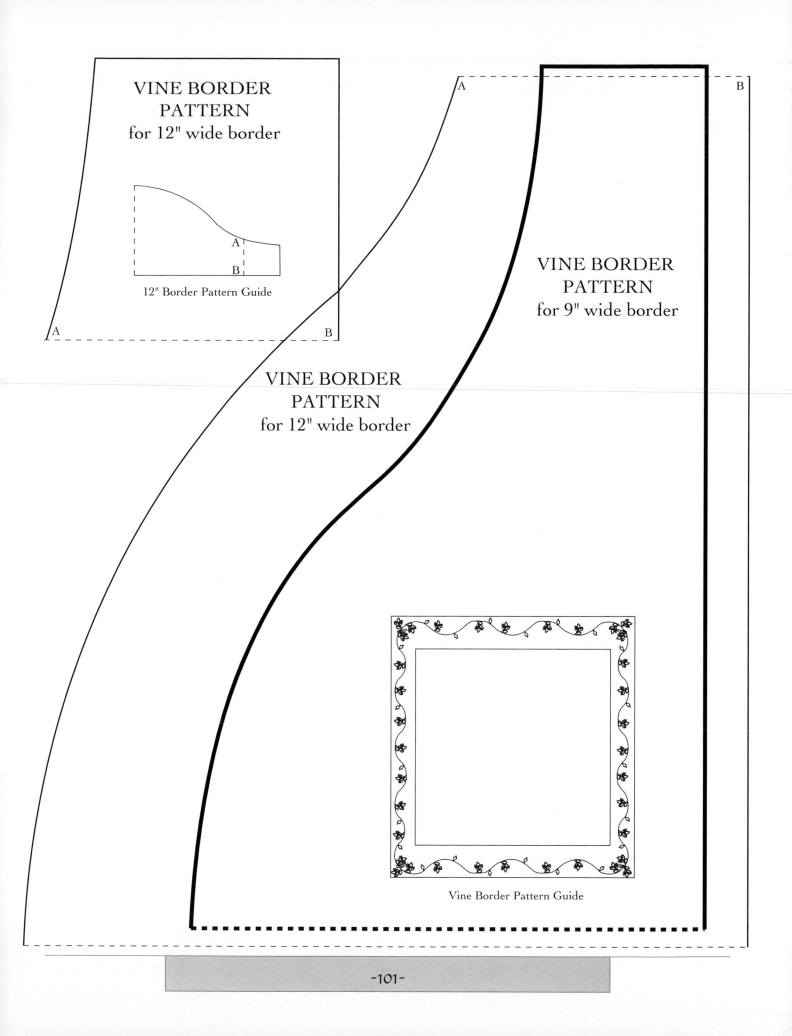

VINE BORDER
PATTERN
for 12" wide border

A

B

12" Border Pattern Guide

VINE BORDER
PATTERN
for 9" wide border

VINE BORDER
PATTERN
for 12" wide border

A

B

Vine Border Pattern Guide

1a
cut 18 and
cut 18 reverse

cut out

Bud
2b
cut 36

2b

1a

cut out

3c

Pattern Guide

4d
cut 11 and
cut 11 reverse

3c
bud color
cut 36
(lay under bud)

Amy's Wedding Quilt. *90" x 96". 1992. Made by the author. Quilted by Katie Born-treger. This large block was inspired by a multi-block quilt made in 1870 by 16-year-old Mary Parks Lawrence in Russellville, KY. The pattern for this quilt is shown on page 85. Photo: Richard Walker.*

Chapter 4
An Analysis of the Findings of State Quilt Documentation Projects

AN OVERVIEW OF MY RESEARCH PROCEDURES

Since 1989 I have surveyed 30 state quilt search projects and 108 museum collections to determine whether large 4-block pieced or appliquéd quilts were a natural progression from earlier whole-cloth and medallion quilt styles and whether they had a regional origin. My research focused on the first 13 colonies and states admitted to the Union before 1850. Thirty states and Washington, D.C. with completed or on-going documentation projects were reviewed. When state documentation was lacking, the largest museum collections were surveyed.

Of those state projects and museums responding to questionnaires, 391 of 51,295 quilts, or 0.76% were constructed in the large 4-block style. An additional 58 quilts from private collections were found and evaluated. Results showed the 4-block style/set occurred no earlier than whole-cloth and medallion quilts, but emerged during the early decades of the 19th century, as did quilts with nine or more smaller blocks repeated across the quilt top.

AN OVERVIEW OF MY FINDINGS

The statistics on the following page pertain to the total quilts found within the 30 states entering the Union before 1850, and also, 108 museum collections within states where state project data was lacking. All types of quilts were included in the total count, whole-cloth, appliquéd, pieced, and tied. Therefore, the percentages look especially small. For example, Ohio found 140 appliquéd quilts made between 1834 and 1900. Since 70 were found to be made in the 4-block style/set, the percentage is 50%; when compared to the total number (7000) quilts found of all style/sets, i.e., whole-cloth, medallion, multiple block, or Log Cabin, the percentage of 4-block quilts drops to 1%. I think this percentage gives a more accurate insight into the phenomena, "Yes, I've seen large 4-block quilts, but now that I think about it, not very often."

Presently, these statistics reveal that about 1 in 132 quilts made in the first 30 states entering the Union (plus Washington, D.C.), were made in the large 4-block style/set.

ROOTS OF THE AMERICAN 4-block QUILTMAKER

Factors contributing to the emergence of this setting/style seem to be emigration and

Sources and General Data

	Total Quilts Found	4-Block Quilts	Documented Percentages
State Projects	46,563	336	0.72%
Museums	4,732	55	1.16%
Total	51,295	391	0.76%

Significance: About 1 in 132 quilts made before 1900 were in the 4-block set.

Projects with Largest Numbers of 4-block Quilts Found

State	Four-Block Quilts	Total Quilts	Documented Percentages
Pennsylvania	123*	1942	6.33%
Ohio	70	7000	1.00%
Illinois	25	15808	0.16%
South Carolina	21	3100	0.68%
Georgia	25	6373	0.39%
Tennessee	11	1425	0.77%
Louisiana	10	1850	0.54%
Missouri	7	720	0.97%
North Carolina	6	10,000	0.06%
Kentucky	5**	600	0.83%

* Only 15 of 67 counties have been surveyed as of March 1993.

** 1000 quilts documented but only 600 documentation forms available for review.

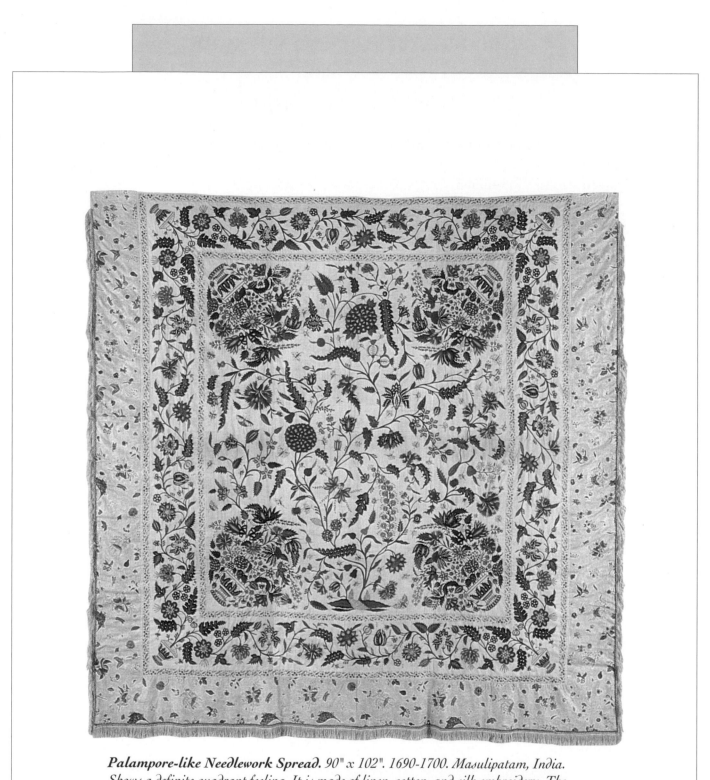

Palampore-like Needlework Spread. *90" x 102". 1690-1700. Masulipatam, India.*
Shows a definite quadrant feeling. It is made of linen, cotton, and silk embroidery. The
chintz border on three sides was added about the last half of the 18th century. The center
and first border are embroidered with the chain stitch to be Palampore-like. Authentic
Palampores were dye painted especially with the Tree of Life design or other center motif.
This piece was intended for the Dutch Holland export market. It was bought in Europe by
an American antiques dealer. Photo: Colonial Williamsburg Foundation.

migration patterns, access to ports of trade, and economic circumstances.

Early exploration of what finally became the first 13 English colonies was done independently by England, France, and Holland. Private trading and commercial venture companies such as the Virginia Company of London, the Massachusetts Bay Co., and the Dutch West India Co. brought not only English families seeking the opportunity for religious freedom and land, but also Scots-Irish Protestants fleeing political and religious persecution. In the 1720's, these settlers began to be joined by thousands of German Lutherans, who brought with them the love for nature's beauty, bounty, and diversity, and the artistry and skills needed to produce Fraktur folk art.

My findings indicate that the large 4-block appliqué quilt was more likely to have been constructed first and foremost by those of German descent, and secondly by Scots-Irish immigrants to Pennsylvania and the Carolinas or women influenced by the German Fraktur style of decoration.

As these peoples moved within the United States, their designs spread with them. The 18th to early 19th century migration trails of Protestant Germans of Pennsylvania, Scots-Irish Presbyterians, some Quakers, and a few Catholics led to inland settlements in Ohio, Illinois, Tennessee, and Missouri, as well as the Carolinas and Georgia on the eastern and southern seaboard, where proportionately, many 4-block quilts were found.

DISPERSAL AND GROWTH OF THE 4-BLOCK SEEDS

In addition to emigration and migration patterns, access to ports of trade and economic circumstances played an important role in the development of the 4-block quilt style. In order for a large 4-block quilt to be made, large pieces of fabrics had to be available. Only if they had access to a loom capable of producing home-spun cloth 24 inches or more in width could quilters weaving their own fabric choose to make a quilt with four large squares or rectangles, as well as even smaller blocks for an appliqué quilt. By 1689 seaports were established on almost the entire length of the east coast at Plymouth, Chesapeake Bay, Hudson Bay, Delaware Bay, Charleston, and Savannah, making possible the importing of textiles.

The textile industry in both America and England began to be mechanized by the last quarter of the 18th century. The cotton gin was invented in 1792–93, and machine spun cotton thread in the early 19th century led to a decline of home produced linen. Shortly after 1800, Ohio textile production became mechanized. Cloth production boomed by the 1830's. Still, between 1820 and 1860, one-third of all imports from England were textiles.[6]

England's East India Company had been supplying silks and cottons but they had become so in demand that attempts were being made to produce them in western countries. England provided special bounties for planting mulberry trees, the fruit of which was to be used as food for the imported silkworm. Charters were issued for ventures in New Jersey, the Carolinas, and Georgia to produce silk for thread, but none were successful. Attempts were also made to create similar effects using domestic textiles. Woolen crewel yarn spun from sheep's wool was used for embroidering designs like those found on Indian prints.

In time, the problem was solved by changes in taste. Chintz cottons, which were relatively cheaper than silk, became stylish. Chintz whole-cloth, medallion style, or cut-out Chintz appliqué quilts were the "high style" bedroom furnishings of the New England and Atlantic seaboard states from about 1820, until fading from glory around 1850,

and it appears that they and whole-cloth quilts may have been the predecessors of the 4-block quilt, which soon spread its wings of diverse variation. The 4-block style/set blossomed between the 1820's and 1870's. Medallion quilts continued to be made during the mid-19th century but waned in popularity as quiltmakers were ready to explore styles and sets other than the wholecloth and medallion quilts.

People and fabrics moved about the country. The midwest became an alluvial plain of sorts where the three colonial cultural regions came together: New England, the Midlands, and the South. Scots-Irish Presbyterian settlers came via the Pennsylvania (Forbes) Road, continuing by boat. New England migrants from Connecticut, Massachusetts, and Vermont traveled to the Western or Connecticut Reserve further inland. Once the Ohio-Erie Canal was built between 1825–1832, Irish and German canal laborers became permanent settlers.[7] All Americans' lives changed when the Baltimore-Ohio (B&O) Railroad charter was issued in 1827. Freight only was carried at first, then in 1859, passengers. To Native Americans, it was the "Iron Horse that belched smoke"; to frontier quilters and general store proprietors, it was the mail order fabric store.

When quilters couldn't or didn't weave their background material, if economically feasible, they would buy it from a merchant, providing he could get it. Relatively easy access to ports of trade would naturally keep the merchant's transportation expenses down. But flatboats and barges floating on navigable interior rivers were the only access some people had to yard goods.

Ohio quilters benefited from ever

Anna M. Siltmann Spoede. 1835–1910.
My paternal great-great grandmother spinning wool.
My dad could remember the old log house being torn
down when he lived in the house behind it.

expanding road systems stretching across the state.[8] Originating in the Conestoga Creek region of Lancaster County, Pennsylvania, during the 18th century, the horse-drawn freight Conestoga wagon could carry up to six tons of merchandise. It was the forerunner of the Prairie Schooner wagon which brought thousands of immigrants to the inland states. The Pennsylvania (Forbes Road) provided access to the western frontier, Ohio and beyond.

Established by 1760, the Great Wagon Road, starting at the Schuylkill River in Philadelphia, was used by most of the first German immigrants going to North Carolina in the mid 1800's. After 1725, available land in Pennsylvania was very scarce, so a southern migration developed. This 735 mile road crossed the Susquehanna River, passed through Maryland, Virginia, North Carolina, and South Carolina, and finally followed the Savannah River in Augusta, Georgia.[9]

By 1817, the Cumberland or National Road was complete from northwest Maryland through southwest Pennsylvania to the Ohio border at Wheeling, West Virginia. By the late 1830's, women in southwest Springfield, Ohio, had much easier access to fabric. The Cumberland Gap, located near the point where Kentucky, Virginia, and Tennessee meet, is where Daniel Boone blazed the Wilderness Road in 1769.

Even in America's pre-Revolutionary years, east coast and mid-Atlantic immigrants sought free fertile lands of the interior. Crossing the Allegheny Mountains through the Cumberland Gap made migration possible all the way to the Mississippi River and opened the Northwest territory to settlement. Besides this northeast route to the interior,

early French emigrés came to the Louisville, Kentucky area from the south via the Mississippi River at New Orleans.

After 1776, the Ohio River brought many German migrants from New England and the mid-Atlantic states through Pittsburgh. The importance of the Ohio and Mississippi Rivers in providing an exchange of goods from the northeastern states to the Gulf of Mexico and back is paramount. In my study I discovered inland quilts with similar characteristics that had documented provenance indicating they had been made hundreds of miles apart. It wasn't until the Louisiana Purchase in 1803, that future midwest states would benefit from the Missouri River connection to trade centers in our country and abroad.

Rose in the Wilderness, detail.
Drawing of one block of the Rose in the Wilderness quilt.
Courtesy of North Carolina Quilt Project.

Whig Rose. *63" x 78". Before 1860. Made in Iowa.*
This quilt could also be categorized as a transition quilt because of its two half-blocks.
Author's collection. Photo: Richard Walker.

Chapter 5
A Closer Look at States with Many 4-Block Quilts

Pennsylvania
COMMEMORATIVE 4-BLOCK EAGLE QUILTS

William Penn received his charter in the last quarter of the 17th century (1681) from King Charles II to settle the region of Pennsylvania. He brought a group of Quakers seeking to establish a colony based on a government of popular will and religious tolerance. Experiments in democratic forms of government encouraged other ethnic immigrants to settle in Pennsylvania in large blocks. Rhineland and southern Germans settled in great numbers in the inland counties of Lancaster, Lehigh Berks, and Northampton. English, Scots-Irish, French, Welsh, Cornish, and Irish also settled the state, but by the American Revolution, one third of the state was populated by German settlers, who were so numerous they became known as the Pennsylvania Dutch (Deutsche). Some integrated well into area communities; others wanted to settle in counties west of the English and German areas. This group settled along the western frontier. By this time it had quickly become a keystone area, integrating first the older colonies of the Northeast and the South, and later the states of the East with the developing territories and states of the Midwest. Along with developing road systems, the three major ports of call were at Philadelphia, Pittsburgh, and Erie, with the Delaware, Susquehanna, Allegheny, Monongahela, and Ohio Rivers used as supplemental connections throughout the state and beyond its borders in all directions, thus providing transportation of yard goods, as well as other necessities.

Princess Feather. *91" x 93". c. 1860-1870. German maker. Notice the stylized oak leaves and tulips in the center. Photo: Courtesy of Philadelphia Museum of Art.*

As previously stated, quilters of Pennsylvania German heritage in this study made more quilts in the 4-block style/set than their counterparts in other states. This holds true for the four most popular 4-block patterns described in Chapter 1.

Common Pennsylvania-German characteristics found were hanging diamond background cross-hatching; brightly colored backgrounds often orange-yellow instead of white; undulating, quilted or appliquéd feather vines in borders or appliquéd vines with flowers; buds and/or birds; eight-pointed stars; Fraktur-style tulips; fruits of nature – oak leaves, trees, urns of flowers; and finally, an inner border of triangles (or often just a narrow unpieced border) to define the 4-block center field. See the PRINCESS FEATHER quilt, page 111. Oak leaves, either quilted or appliquéd symbolized happiness, stability, and long life. According to Anita Schorsch, "Western culture has kept them as a symbol of life, a gift of grace either as the Old Testament Tree of Knowledge or the New Testament Tree of Life. The dove shaped bird meant the Holy Spirit of the Trinity or the Annunciation of Mary. The eagle was to bring believers closer to God, and finally, the rose or lily (tulip as it was later known as), was a symbol for Mary."[10] During Martin Luther's Reformation, the heart became a predominant symbol for abundance. Pennsylvania-Germans felt the heart also represented divine and amorous love and often reserved the motif for the special bridal quilt.

A special design very unique to Pennsylvania must be recognized. The Eagle quilts found mostly in Pennsylvania were most likely made to commemorate our country's first centennial through Philadelphia's Centennial Exposition in 1876. Historian Ruth Finley found some of these quilts were called "Union"; and suggested that the single eagle pattern was fleetingly revived by northern sympathizers in the 1860's from the Revolutionary War Eagle quilt predecessors. In actuality, the few "Lone Eagle" quilts found before 1860 were probably patriotic responses to the Mexican War of 1846–1848. Only one 4-block Eagle quilt from Pennsylvania found in this survey was made between 1860 and 1865. The other ten were made between 1870 and 1890. Eleven 4-block Eagle quilts found were from Pennsylvania, three from Ohio, one from New Jersey.

STENCIL OR CUT-OUT APPLIQUÉ DESIGNS

The German art of ornamental paper cutting, scherenschnitte, became an original source for beautiful cut-out appliqué patterns. Tinkers, traveling tin salesman, could pay for a night's dinner and lodging with a pierced and cut tin stencil, paper cut-work appliqué patterns, or quilting stencils. See quilts on pages 27 and 118.

Ohio

RED AND GREEN 4-BLOCK QUILTS

Quilts in Community: Ohio's Traditions by Ricky Clark, George W. Knepper, and Ellice Ronsheim was written after the project documented 7,000 quilts. In the chapter "German Aesthetics, Germanic Communities" Ricky Clark reveals that about one-half of the 140 appliqué quilts found in the Ohio project made between 1834 and 1900 were in the quadrant, 4-block style/setting.

Migrating Pennsylvania-German Protestants and some Catholics, popularized red and green floral appliqué in mid 19th century Ohio. The style/setting most favored included wide multiple borders around the center area, ending frequently with a high-contrasting colorful binding. Floral appliqué reached its peak in Ohio between 1850 and 1860. Statistics show that of the 140 appliqué quilts made between 1834 and 1900, 42 or 30% were ethnic German-made (meaning immigrant or first generation American); and of 74 quilts with the ethnic background of the maker known, 42 or 57% were made by Germanic women. These statistics are especially meaningful when considering the 1850 census – only 6% of the population were immigrants from Germany, and 10% Germans from Pennsylvania. See *Quilts in Community: Ohio's Traditions* by Clark, Knepper and Ronsheim, Rutledge Hill Press.

Illinois
CANALS, LAKES, RIVERS, AND ROADS BRING 4-BLOCK QUILTMAKERS

The area we now know as Illinois was controlled by France until 1763, when Great Britain gained control after the French and Indian Wars. With the 1779 capture of the British seat of government in Kaskaskia, Illinois became a county of Virginia. After first being part of the Northwest territory, then Indiana territory, the Illinois territory finally gained statehood in 1818. Very early Anglo-Saxon British Isles settlers came from Virginia, Kentucky, and Tennessee to southern Illinois. Northwestern Germans emmigrated to Illinois and Missouri as early as 1832. According to Cheryl Wieburg Kennedy, Director of the Early American Museum of Mahomet, Illinois, and the Illinois Quilt Research Project, many 1840's northern Illinois communities were settled by direct German immigrants and Pennsylvania-Germans who had come from Pennsylvania, North Carolina, and Ohio via the Erie Canal, the Great Lakes, the Ohio River, and the National Road. Other New Englanders and New Yorkers of Scots-Irish descent also came by this northern route. See the PIECED BLAZING STAR quilt, page 114.

The Royal area (Champaign County), German Valley, Stephenson County, southeastern Wabash County, and Emden are among many other areas and communities that were settled by German families. Many came not only for the freedom to enjoy political or religious beliefs but for simple economic opportunities including freedom from unstable financial conditions, overwhelming taxes, agriculture and industrial depression, and very poor labor wages. English, Scots, and Welsh immigrants cited the latter reasons, while the Irish and lower Rhineland Germans added famine to the list because of the late 1840's potato crop failure.

During one three-year period in the early 1850's, more than 500,000 Germans immigrated to America, resulting in a 1.5% reduction in Germany's population. Even today many family names can be traced back to the East Frisiam (Ostfiesen) area of Germany as well as the Rhine Valley. Documentation papers from the Illinois Quilt Research Project revealed many mid-19th century Illinois residents could trace their families back to Pennsylvania. The 1860 Illinois Census reported more than 80,000 Pennsylvanians had moved to Illinois.[11] In the 1840's the vast number of European immigrants began and continued through World War 1. See the STAR SPANGLED BANNER quilt, page 28.

Pieced Blazing Star. *96" x 96". c. 1855. Made by Mary Elizabeth Byron Fortenbaugh in Halifax, Pennsylvania. Now owned by Illinois State Museum, Springfield, IL. Photo: Marlin Ross.*

South Carolina
ORIGINALITY IN FEATHERS, ROSES, AND PINEAPPLES

Charleston, South Carolina, and Georgia quiltmakers had a greater supply of fabrics to choose from because of the way South Carolina's coastline accommodated large ships. Charleston was also a port of entry for countless immigrants; first English, then largely Scots-Irish and German. In *Social Fabric: South Carolina's Traditional Quilts* by Laurel Horton and Lynn Robertson Myers, Laurel's chapter "Quiltmaking Traditions in South Carolina" states that even though there were outside influences on the traditions of the settled German community, these quiltmakers continued to use "certain recognizable German characteristics, such as predilection toward all-over visual designs even when using a block pattern, a strong preference for designs with diagonal lines, a marked orderliness even when using many different fabrics, and a preference for yellow as a unifying color.[12]

Other European ethnic groups were also represented, but here as well as up through the Virginia coast, the West Indies and especially African cultural heritages become significant factors in the amount of leisure time a woman had to pursue quiltmaking. According to Horton, an assimilation of ethnic German and Scots-Irish aesthetic principles is the reason that German-occupied Piedmont area quilts differ from those of the coastal plain. With Laurel's help, thirty-two 4-block quilts were found in the South Carolina project, 21 of which fell within my cut-off date of 1900. These 32 quilts show more original interpretations of commonly seen 4-block patterns such as the Princess Feather and Whig Rose.

Also, an original Pineapple pattern was found to be extremely regional in nature with three other extremely similar quilts within South Carolina, and five in other states; one each in Virginia, Georgia, Mississippi, and two in Texas. See the PINEAPPLE quilt, page 116. My collection includes a much simpler version of this appliquéd pineapple from South Carolina.

More pieced 4-block quilts were also found here than any other state (11), with the possible exception of Pennsylvania. See the PINEAPPLE quilt, page 36 and the ROCKY MOUNTAIN quilt, page 37.

Georgia
AND THE SOUTHERN COASTAL STATES

Georgia was the youngest of the first 13 colonies in that England claimed the territory, but did not effectively settle it until 1732. It was much larger then since it included most of our present-day states of Alabama and Mississippi. See the EGYPTIAN DESIGN quilt, page 37.

Austria-Bavarian (Salzburg) Germans settled in New Ebenezer and Savannah, Georgia, while the Scottish Highlanders went to Darien, and New England Congregationalists went to Sundury and Midway. The Atlantic Ocean coastline had the most settlements by 1752. In the early decades of the 1800's, when plantations were firmly established, the beastly temperatures and humidity during the Savannah summers became vacation time for wealthy families to go to the southern highlands or northern cities of Boston, New York, or Philadelphia. Vacationing several weeks "up north" most likely afforded the opportunity to exchange

Pineapple. 61½" x 79½". c. 1890-1910. Made by Margaret Bell Kelly, Simpson County, MS. Backing is pieced from corn sacks printed twice with the corn ear logo "Full Weight," "Corn Meal," and "Florence, Miss." Steen's Creek became Florence in 1901, so either the top is older than the backing material or the quilt was made after 1901. Owned by Mississippi State Historical Museum, Jackson, MS. Photo: Collection of Mississippi State Historical Museum.

and copy 4-block patterns.[13] Anita Weinraub, the Georgia quilt documentation project director has commented that there is still a strong Scots-Irish Presbyterian heritage within the state, followed secondly by a Baptist heritage.

Alas, very few large 4-block quilts were found in Mississippi and Alabama. Considering the Louisiana project found about 10 and Georgia about 25, as yet, no plausible explanation other than that migrating Pennsylvania and South Carolina Germans and Scots-Irish didn't settle or stay long in these areas. It should be noted that when Georgia was admitted into the Union in 1783, Mississippi and Alabama were considered "Territories South of the Ohio River." They had been given to England by the 1763 Treaty of Paris at the end of the French and Indian Wars. In the 1770's both future states were greatly populated by migrant settlers seeking refuge from the ever-growing unrest with the British crown rule on the eastern seaboard. Since 1682, France had long claimed New Orleans as a port of entry.

In 1731, Louisiana became a French crown colony. Besides French settlers, thousands of Germans settled on the river just above New Orleans in an area known as the "German Coast." In a secret treaty of 1762, Louisiana and New Orleans were ceded to Spain. By 1783 Spain controlled most of the remaining Louisiana territory which encompassed nearly all areas west of the Mississippi River. In 1800, Spain ceded this vast area back to France. It was only three years later that President Thomas Jefferson authorized the Louisiana Purchase to expand America's holding.[14] See the PINEAPPLE quilt, on page 116. Its name is Pineapple and it was made in Mississippi, but this same design is known as Alabama Beauty in Alabama

Louisiana held a strategic command on commerce within the interior simply because the Mississippi River, draining the continental interior, flowed through here to the Gulf of Mexico. This one geographical fact had great impact on quilting in the Midwest: quiltmakers' choice of fabric was based on financial circumstances and availability of materials. After availability, choices of patterns were determined by need for a utilitarian or fancy quilt. If need allowed a special fancy quilt, then originality, personal ethnic heritage, or a neighbor's influential heritage largely determined the pattern to be used.

Tennessee
"TINKER" STENCIL-CUT 4-BLOCK APPLIQUÉS

Virginians were the first émigrés led into this part of what was formerly western North Carolina by Thomas Walker in 1750. William Bean was the first permanent white settler to build his cabin along the Watauga River in 1768. By 1780, Nashborough, (Nashville) was established. North Carolina finally ceded the territory to the U. S. government in 1789. Morristown, Tennessee, was settled by Scots-Irish immigrants. They came down the Holston River from the Cumberland Gap. If they turned north, they went into Kentucky; if they turned south, they went to Morristown. Some Pennsylvania Germans came after the Civil War. Perhaps Germantown, Tennessee, was named by settlers from Germantown, Pennsylvania. By 1789, hundreds of settlers were coming into the area. The Revolutionary War was over, and some were ready to strike out for new lands; the land bonuses and lotteries given as payment for some who took part in the war had not proven successful. They were ready to try again. Physically, Tennessee stretches from the Appalachian Mountain boundary with North Carolina in the east all the way to where the Mississippi Rivers borders Missouri and Arkansas. It tended to be a state through which people immigrated. Only 112 miles wide, people in Kentucky, Virginia, Georgia, Alabama, and Mississippi readily passed through. See KENTUCKY TOBACCO LEAF AND TULIP STENCIL quilt, page 31. Perhaps Tennessee's migrant-oriented nature explains why it was not affected much by the European immigrant waves during the second to third quarter of the 19th century. Conversely, this nature provided for a mixture and exchange of quilting styles and preferences.

Peddler's Quilt (Cut-out Appliqué). *83" x 66". c. 1860-1870. Made by Arminta Byers Cox in Tennessee. Documentation form indicates "a peddler pinched out the pattern for the maker." Collection of Peggy Craig. Photo: Courtesy of The Quilts of Tennessee.*

A number of 4-block scherenschnitte-like, stencil-cut appliqué quilts were documented in the Tennessee Project. Traveling salesmen/tin buyers and tinkers could turn scrap pieces of tin roofing into profit when they cut out a quilting or appliqué design. Only one such 4-block quilt was found in this study outside Tennessee. It is pictured in the Vermont project book, *Plain and Fancy: Vermont's People And Their Quilts As A Reflection of America* by Cleveland and Bister. No other states or museums reported large 4-block quilts with these "Snowflake" cut-out patterns, with the exception of the scherenschnitte-like quilts found in Pennsylvania. See CUT-OUT APPLIQUÉ quilt, page 27.

Missouri
THE NEW RHINELAND FOR EMMIGRATING GERMANS

Ste. Genevieve was the first Missouri settlement established by French explorers in 1735, followed by Pierre Laclede from New Orleans thirty years later at St. Louis. Marthasville was the first settled village established in what was to become Warren County (west of St. Louis). The famous fur trader Indian Phillips came as an employee of a fur company in 1763, followed by Choteau and Lozie, who received grants from the Spanish government for a large tract of land in the present counties of Warren and St. Charles. Daniel Boone's son-in-law, Flanders Callaway, bought the grants, and in 1795, established Callaway Post several miles west of Marthasville. Settlements in central Warren County date back to 1808, with the coming of Thomas Kennedy of Virginia, Anthony Keeler of Pennsylvania, Samuel Gibson of South Carolina, and Daniel McCoy and

David Boyd of Kentucky.[15] In this pioneer period, Marthasville was the principal landing place for all the territory. It was the only avenue of marketing by boat for receiving goods and exporting farmers' produce. This shipping interest was a big business for the area.[16] Cotton was very successfully raised and produced some of the clothing needs of the families. Flax was also raised, chiefly for the bark of which linen and linsey were made. "A flax patch and a flock of sheep were the pride of every family, and the lady who was an expert flax spinner and weaver, was the envy of her sex, and had the admiration of the opposite sex."[17]

By the time of the Louisiana Purchase from France in 1803, among the 10,000 French settlers from Illinois country were Virginians and émigrés from Kentucky and Tennessee, who then became the major immediate source for continued settlement until 1820. Immigrants came from Germany, Ireland, and England via the Mississippi. In about 1824, Gottfried Duden thoroughly traveled through the Warren County area. When Duden returned to Germany, he wrote a book describing what he'd seen so accurately that when immigrants settled in this area, they already knew many places and scenes as they came to them.

Some societies came to Missouri en masse such as the Berlin Society in 1833, to St. Charles, followed by the Gissen Society in 1834. "No other class of people ever did more for the development of the country, or made better or more thrifty citizens than the Germans. They caused the hillsides to blossom with fruit and opened large farms in the midst of the dense forest. Villages and towns sprang up where solitude had reigned, and the liberal arts began to flourish."[18] The greatest influx of German immigrants to Marthasville began in 1834, principally from New Orleans up the Mississippi River.

The German Settlement Society of Pennsylvania was organized in Philadelphia on Aug. 27, 1863, for the purpose of founding a German colony where language and customs could be preserved in the new country. Scouts were sent out to locate suitable areas. George F. Bayer was the agent hired to buy the land, lay out the town, and start the new colony of Hermann, (later to become Hermann, Missouri, in Gasconade, County.)[19] My own paternal great-grandparents, John Gerhard Spoede (Spöde is the German spelling) and his new bride of three weeks, Anna M. Siltmann, made the journey from New Orleans to St. Louis, Missouri, in September 1855.

By the beginning of the Civil War in 1860, so many Germans had settled on the bluffs and uplands south of the Missouri River as well as both in St. Louis and further west, that the area became known as the "Missouri Rhineland." In "Characteristics of Missouri-German Quilts," *(Uncoverings, 1984)* Suellen Meyers discovered distinctive styles and characteristics of Missouri-German made quilts from communities along the lower Missouri River that had been settled virtually by German immigrants alone.

During the next decade, more immigrants came from Ohio, Illinois, and Indiana than from the upper south. Still more Germans came, settling this time in Kansas City as well as St. Louis. Like Tennessee, Missouri saw many migrant populations passing through its borders. Missouri's borders touch Iowa, Illinois, Kentucky, Tennessee, Arkansas,

Oklahoma, Kansas, and Nebraska.

Until Texas was admitted in 1845, Missouri was the westernmost state of the Union. For decades it served as the beginning of the Sante Fe and Oregon Trails bringing tens of thousands of explorers and settlers deeper into the frontier. St. Louis was the new western frontier's only contact with the culture of the East, while Easterners thought of Missouri as the "Gateway to the West." Throughout Missouri's early years of settlement and after, the importance of being bordered and transgressed by the Mississippi and Missouri rivers respectively allowed not only the east to meet the west, but also the north to meet the south. Headwaters of the Mississippi begin in Minnesota and drain into the gulf of Mexico. With its headwaters in Oregon, the Missouri River flows half-way across the United States before converging with the Mississippi on the Missouri-Illinois border. The Ohio river starts in Pennsylvania and converges with the Mississippi at the point where Missouri borders Illinois and Kentucky. See SUNBURST STAR, page 33.

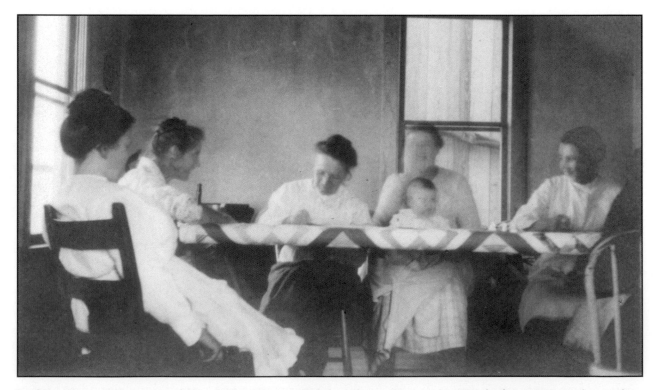

Quilting Party. *Front room of Mr. & Mrs. Herman Redeker's home, Warrenton, MO, built in 1912. (Left to right) Mrs. George (Mayme) Hess, Mrs. Herman (Maggie) Redeker, my paternal great-grandmother, Mrs. I.N. Rhine, Hilda Spoede holding Mina Hess, and my grandmother, Melinda Redeker, 16 years old.*

North Carolina
Princess Feather Pattern Preferred in Southwest Piedmont

North Carolina did not have a safe coastline or a large harbor to accept many European immigrants and trade ships from the Caribbean. Therefore, her first settlers in 1610, were Englishmen migrating south from the greatly expanding Jamestown, Virginia, colony, to take advantage of the rich bottom lands of the Carolinas. Trade products at this time could only move north into Virginia and New England to be sold or reshipped to world markets. Small, shallow keel English ships could dock at Petersburg or Norfolk, Virginia.

By 1663, French, German, and Swiss colonists were migrating from Virginia and the Abermarle region of North Carolina, south down the Pamlico and Neuse Rivers. After 1718, when Indian and pirate threats had been quelled, the lower Cape Fear region became home to those migrating north from Charleston, South Carolina, a major port of debarkation for European, Caribbean, and African immigrants.

The Upper Cape Fear area of Campbelltown (now Fayetteville) was settled by thousands of Scottish immigrants fleeing British persecution after the ill-fated 40-minute Battle of Culloden in 1746. By 1750, migration from Philadelphia towards the interior Piedmont region was led by large populations of Protestant Germans and Scots-Irish Presbyterians who had fled religious persecution in Germany and Ulster (Northern Ireland). Finding very little and very costly land prompted them to venture south. This arduous migration trail, aptly named the Great Road, started in Philadelphia, Pennsylvania, and ended in the North Carolina counties of Yadking, Catawba, Person, and Pender via the Yadkin, Catawba, and Neuse Rivers headwaters. Trade to and from these interior settlements was accomplished through Charleston, South Carolina; Augusta, Georgia; Knoxville, Tennessee; Baltimore and Philadelphia. The population in 1760 totaled 130,000 with a break down of ethnic groups as follows: 45,000 English, 40,000 Scots, and 15,000 Germans.[20]

Eventually, the Scots-Irish would be the largest ethnic group. German immigrants after 1790, didn't readily settle in North Carolina. Instead, the many thousands of German immigrants went on to the midwest and larger cities during the period from about 1830–1850. The use of the German

Cotton Boll, detail. *Block detail drawn from quilt. Courtesy of the North Carolina Quilt Project.*

language itself and the resulting isolation it caused was largely responsible for this migration. However, those families that stayed did learn English around 1825.[21] Despite their language barriers the German quiltmakers evidently influenced the Scots-Irish quiltmakers here in at least one pattern and setting: the 4-block Princess Feather. Perhaps the comparatively small numbers of Germans versus the other ethnic populations can explain why approximately only 1 in 1500 quilts made in North Carolina before 1900 were in the 4-block style/set. Sullivan offers other valid reasons for German influence on North Carolina's quiltmaking, which in the case of the 4-block quilt, might also account

for their rarity in North Carolina.[22]

The earliest surviving documented North Carolina Project quilts were chintz, either the cut-out, pieced, or appliquéd medallion style. They came from the Piedmont counties, Mecklenburg, Carbarrus, Iredell, Davie, and McDowell. Mecklenburg was the center for Scots-Irish settlements. The height of popularity for this style quilt was from 1820 to about 1850. As noted in Laurel Horton's thesis, "Economic Influences on German and Scots-Irish Quilts in Antebellun Rown County, North Carolina" (Chapel Hill: University of North Carolina, 1979): some quilts made in North Carolina German communities settled before 1860 had decidedly different appearances from quilts made by Scots-Irish descendants in neighboring counties.[23] During this same period before the Civil War, square blocks of repeated appliqués emerged as a new style. So did the 4-block quadrant arrangement.

No matter whether they came as immigrants from Europe or migrants from Pennsylvania or South Carolina, women of all ages surely admired one another's quilts, exchanged patterns, and remembered favorite quilts of their grandmother's for later reproduction to help alleviate the arduous, tedious days and months of traveling. This could account for the fact that very similar quilts were found in counties separated by hundreds of miles. When several adjacent settlements (now counties), were populated by ethnic immigrants and migrants, the same reasoning holds true. For example, the North Carolina Project found more Princess Feather quilts originating in the southwest Piedmont counties of Cleveland, Gaston, Lincoln, and Catawba than anywhere else.

Whig Rose, detail. *89" x 90". 1850. Made in Pennsylvania, now owned by Mary Schafer, Michigan. Photo: The Keva Partnership.*

Kentucky
POLITICAL BATTLE LEAVES ROSE IN THE MIDDLE

Native-born statesman Henry Clay, and Kentucky raised Zachary Taylor, played a part in the often used 4-block pattern called "Whig Rose" or "Democrat Rose." Clay was a staunch member of the Whig political party from its infant beginnings of opposition to the federal Alien and Sedition Acts of 1798, (which was the government's attempt to control criticism against slaveholders and businessmen by farmers who used the Mississippi River for transporting goods to New Orleans) to the party's formal organization in 1834. Could Kentucky women have named this rose in honor of a native son arguing against slavery and for the well-being of the common man? See WHIG ROSE, page 122.

Democrat Andrew Jackson and Clay were long-time political enemies. Since the War of 1812, Jackson had become a military hero for his involvement. His native state was South Carolina before working in Nashville, Tennessee, as a lawyer prior to his military career. Could women from these states have named the same pattern "Democrat Rose" for their hero?

By 1840, both names were commonly interchanged. But after Clay's defeat by Democrat James Polk in the Presidential election of 1844, a new pattern emerged named "Whig's Defeat." See WHIG'S DEFEAT, page 36.

Closing Remarks

Rivers, trails, roads, and then railroads moved people and goods across this entire continent. Quiltmakers didn't have to pack their ethnic heritage, but once they unpacked their large 4-block quilts, it came through loud and clear. The beautiful German Fraktur designs applied with newly acquired English quilting skills brought memories to the Pennsylvania German quiltmaker of a homeland far away. In their adopted homeland of America their 4-block quilts would remain legacies of their German heritage.

Democrat Rose, detail. c. 1865. Made by Mrs. Joseph Grigsby Smyth. Block detail drawn from The Democrat Rose Quilt, published in Lone Stars: A Legacy of Texas Quilts, 1836-1936 *by Karoline Patterson Bresenhan and Nancy O'Bryant Puentes, copyright 1986 by the University of Texas Press. Used by permission of authors.*

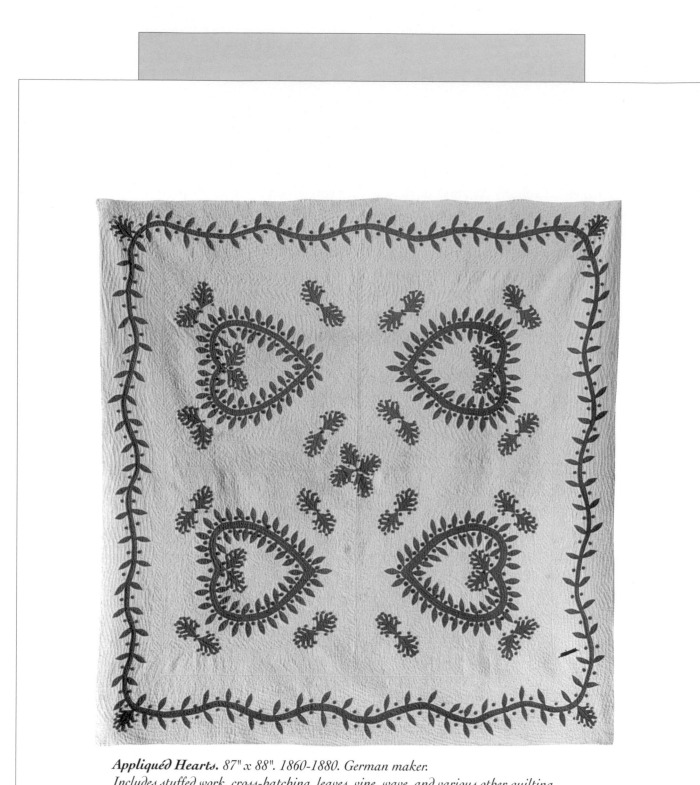

Appliquéd Hearts. *87" x 88". 1860-1880. German maker.*
Includes stuffed work, cross-hatching, leaves, vine, wave, and various other quilting
designs. Photo: Courtesy of the Philadelphia Museum of Art.

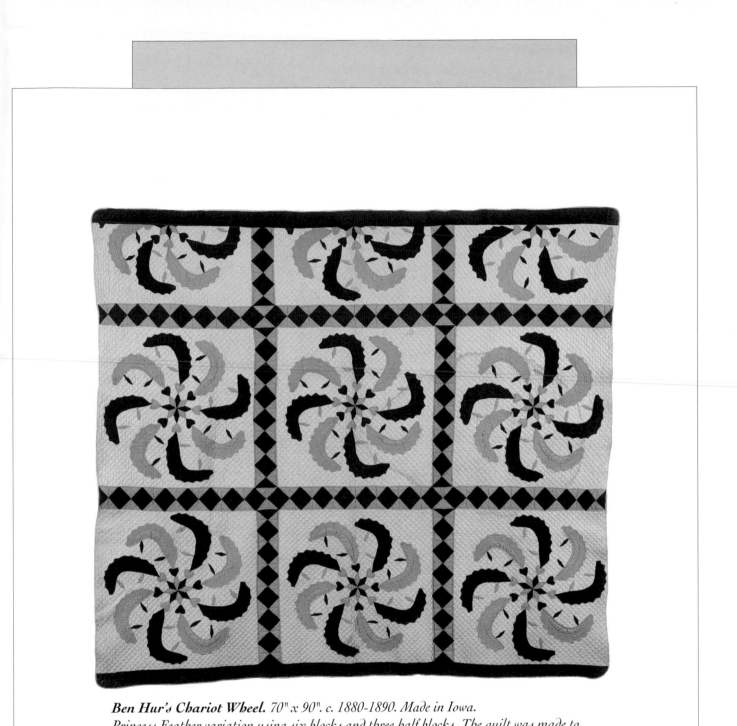

Ben Hur's Chariot Wheel. *70" x 90". c. 1880-1890. Made in Iowa.*
Princess Feather variation using six blocks and three half blocks. The quilt was made to
fit a single bed, and could be considered a transition quilt. Notice the black quilting
thread. Author's collection. Photo: Richard Walker.

Notes & Index

1. Kirkpatrick, Erma Hughes. "Garden Variety Quilts," in *North Carolina Quilts*. Eanes, Ellen Fickling, et al., Ruth Haislip Roberson, ed. (Chapel Hill, North Carolina: The University of North Carolina Press and London, 1988), p. 67.

2. Horton, Laurel. "Textile Traditions in South Carolina's Dutch Fork" in *Bits and Pieces*. Ed. Jeanette Lasansky, et al., (Lewisburg, PA: Oral Traditions Project of the Union County Historical Society, Courthouse, 1991), p. 73.

3. For futher information refer to *New York Beauties: Quilts from the Empire State* by Atkins and Tepper. p. 113–115.

4. *New Encyclopaedia Britannica*, Vol. 8, 1987, p. 566.

5. Schorsch, Anita. *Plain & Fancy: Country Quilts of the Pennsylvania-Germans*. (New York: Sterling Publishing Co., Inc.), p. 27.

6. Ellice Ronsheim. "The Impact of Technology on the Availability of Dress Goods in Ohio" in *Quilts in Community: Ohio's Traditions*. Clark, Knepper and Rosnsheim. (Nashville: Rutledge Hill Press, 1991), p. 57–60.

7. *New Encyclopaedia Britannica*, Vol. 29, 1987, p. 174–175.

8. See "Early Migrants to Ohio" by George W. Knepper for more complete information in *Quilts in Community: Ohio's Traditions*. Clark, Knepper and Ronsheim. (Nashville: Rutledge Hill Press, 1991), p. 9–10, various entries to p. 19.

9. Sullivan, Kathleen. "Pieced and Plentiful" in *Bits and Pieces*. Lasansky. p. 65.

10. Schorsch, p. 35–36.

11. Elbert, Duane. *History from the Heartland: Quilt Paths across Illinois.* (Nashville: Rutledge Hill Press, 1993), pps. 23–25, 42–43, 49.

12. Horton, Laurel. "Quiltmaking Traditions in South Carolina" in *Social Fabric: South Carolina's Traditional Quilts*. Laurel Horton and Lynn Robertson Myer. (McKissick Museum, University of South Carolina), p. 19–21.

13. *New Encyclopaedia Britannica*, Vol. 8, 1987. p. 327.

14. *Ibid.* p. 38.

15. "Brief History of Warren County." *The Warrenton Banner*. Vol. L, No. 19, 18 Dec. 1914, p. 1.

16. "The First Town, Marthasville." *The Warrenton Banner*. Vol. L, No. 19, 18 Dec. 1914, p. 14.

17. "Chief Occupation." *The Warrenton Banner*. Vol. L, No. 19, 18 Dec. 1914, p. 4.

18. "The German Immigration." *The Warrenton Banner*. Vol. L, No. 19, 18 Dec. 1914, p. 2.

19. "Hermann Will Honor Its Founder in Kickoff at Town's Sesquecentennial." *The Warrenton News Journal*. No. 23, April 1986, p. B6.

20. Joines, Joyce. "Making Do," in *North Carolina Quilts*. p. 9–10.

21. Sullivan, Kathleen. *Bits and Pieces*. Lasansky. p. 68.

22. *Ibid.* p. 69–70.

23. Horton, Laurel. "Quiltmaking Traditions in South Carolina." p. 20.

Bibliography

Allen, Rosemary E. *North Country Quilts and Coverlets from Beamish Museum, County Durham.* Beamish. 1987.

Arkansas Quilter's Guild, Inc. *Arkansas Quilts: Arkansas Warmth.* Kentucky: American Quilter's Society, 1987.

Atkins, Jacqueline MN. and Phyllis A. Tepper. *New York Beauties: Quilts from the Empire State.* New York: Penguin Books USA., Inc., 1992.

Bishop, Robert. *New Discoveries in American Quilts.* New York: E. P. Dutton and Co., Inc., 1975.

Brackman, Barbara. *Clues in the Calico: A Guide to Identifying and Dating Antique Quilts.* McLean, Virgina: EPM Publishers, Inc., 1989.

Bresenhan, Karoline Patterson and Nancy O'Bryant Puentes. *Lone Stars–A Legacy of Texas Quilts, 1836-1936.* Texas: University of Texas Press, 1986.

Clark, Ricky, George Knepper, and Ellice Ronsheim. *Quilts in Community: Ohio's Traditions.* Tennessee: Rutledge Hill Press, 1991.

Cleveland, Richard L. and Donna Bister. *Plain and Fancy: Vermont's People and Their Quilts As a Reflection of America.* California: The Quilt Digest Press, 1991.

Elbert, Duane. *History from the Heartland: Quilt Paths across Illinois.* Tennessee: Rutledge Hill Press, 1993.

Finley, John. *Kentucky Quilts 1800-1900: The Kentucky Quilt Project.* New York: Pantheon Books, 1982.

Finley, Ruth. *Old Patchwork Quilts and the Women Who Made Them.* New York: Grosset and Dunlap, 1929.

Gwinner, Schnuppe von. *The History of the Patchwork Quilt–Origins, Traditions and Symbols of a Textile Art.* Pennsylvania: Schiffer Publishing Co., 1988.

Hall, Carrie and Rose Kretsinger. *The Romance of the Patchwork Quilt.* New York: Dover Publishers, Inc., 1988 ed.

Havig, Bettina. *Missouri Heritage Quilts.* Kentucky: American Quilter's Society, 1986.

Horton, Laurel and Lynn Robertson Myer. *Social Fabric: South Carolina's Traditional Quilts.* South Carolina: McKissick Museum.

Jenkins, Susan and Linda Seward. *The American Quilt Story–The How-To and Heritage of a Craft Tradition.* Pennsylvania: Rodale Press, 1991.

Lansansky, Jeanette. *Bits and Pieces–Textile Traditions.* Pennsylvania: Oral Traditions Project of the Union County Historical Society, 1991.

MacDowell, Marsha and Ruth D. Fitrzgerald, eds. *Michigan Quilts–150 Years of a Textile Tradition.* Michigan: Michigan State University Museum, 1987.

Martin, Nancy. *Pieces of the Past.* Washington: That Patchwork Place, Inc., 1986.

Martin, Nancy. *Threads of Time.* Washington: That Patchwork Place, Inc., 1990.

Nelson, Cyril I. and Carter Houck. *Treasury of American Quilts.* New York: Greenwich House, 1982.

Peck, Amelia. *American Quilts and Coverlets in the Metropolitan Museum of Art.* New York: Dutton Studio Books, 1990.

Roberson, Ruth Haislip, ed., et al. *North Carolina Quilts.* North Carolina: The University of North Carolina Press, 1988.

Safford, Carleton L. and Robert Bishop. *America's Quilts and Coverlets.* New York: Bonanza Books, 1985.

Schorsch, Anita. *Plain & Fancy: Country Quilts of the Pennsylvania-Germans.* New York: Sterling/Main Street Books, 1992.

Texas Heritage Quilt Society. *Texas Quilts–Texas Treasures.* Kentucky: American Quilter's Society, 1986.

Webster, Marie. *Quilts: Their Story and How to Make Them.* California: Practical Patchwork, 1990.

American Quilter's Society
dedicated to publishing books for today's quilters

The following AQS publications are currently available:

- **Adapting Architectural Details for Quilts,** Carol Wagner, #2282: AQS, 1991, 88 pages, softbound, $12.95
- **American Beauties: Rose & Tulip Quilts,** Gwen Marston & Joe Cunningham, #1907: AQS, 1988, 96 pages, softbound, $14.95
- **America's Pictorial Quilts,** Caron L. Mosey, #1662: AQS, 1985, 112 pages, hardbound, $19.95
- **Appliqué Designs: My Mother Taught Me to Sew,** Faye Anderson, #2121: AQS, 1990, 80 pages, softbound, $12.95
- **Appliqué Patterns from Native American Beadwork Designs,** Dr. Joyce Mori, #3790: AQS, 1994, 96 pages, softbound, $14.95
- **Arkansas Quilts: Arkansas Warmth,** Arkansas Quilter's Guild, Inc., #1908: AQS, 1987, 144 pages, hardbound, $24.95
- **The Art of Hand Appliqué,** Laura Lee Fritz, #2122: AQS, 1990, 80 pages, softbound, $14.95
- **...Ask Helen More About Quilting Designs,** Helen Squire, #2099: AQS, 1990, 54 pages, 17 x 11, spiral-bound, $14.95
- **Award-Winning Quilts & Their Makers, Vol. I: The Best of AQS Shows – 1985-1987,** #2207: AQS, 1991, 232 pages, softbound, $24.95
- **Award-Winning Quilts & Their Makers, Vol. II: The Best of AQS Shows – 1988-1989,** #2354: AQS, 1992, 176 pages, softbound, $24.95
- **Award-Winning Quilts & Their Makers, Vol. III: The Best of AQS Shows – 1990-1991,** #3425: AQS, 1993, 180 pages, softbound, $24.95
- **Award-Winning Quilts & Their Makers, Vol. IV: The Best of AQS Shows – 1992-1993,** #3791: AQS, 1994, 180 pages, softbound, $24.95
- **Classic Basket Quilts,** Elizabeth Porter & Marianne Fons, #2208: AQS, 1991, 128 pages, softbound, $16.95
- **A Collection of Favorite Quilts,** Judy Florence, #2119: AQS, 1990, 136 pages, softbound, $18.95
- **Creative Machine Art,** Sharee Dawn Roberts, #2355: AQS, 1992, 142 pages, 9 x 9, softbound, $24.95
- **Dear Helen, Can You Tell Me?...All about Quilting Designs,** Helen Squire, #1820: AQS, 1987, 51 pages, 17 x 11, spiral-bound, $12.95
- **Double Wedding Ring Quilts: New Quilts from an Old Favorite,** #3870: AQS, 1994, 112 pages, softbound, $14.95
- **Dye Painting!,** Ann Johnston, #3399: AQS, 1992, 88 pages, softbound, $19.95
- **Dyeing & Overdyeing of Cotton Fabrics,** Judy Mercer Tescher, #2030: AQS, 1990, 54 pages, softbound, $9.95
- **Encyclopedia of Pieced Quilt Patterns,** compiled by Barbara Brackman, #3468: AQS, 1993, 552 pages, hardbound, $34.95
- **Flavor Quilts for Kids to Make: Complete Instructions for Teaching Children to Dye, Decorate & Sew Quilts,** Jennifer Amor, #2356: AQS, 1991, 120 pages, softbound, $12.95
- **From Basics to Binding: A Complete Guide to Making Quilts,** Karen Kay Buckley, #2381: AQS, 1992, 160 pages, softbound, $16.95
- **Fun & Fancy Machine Quiltmaking,** Lois Smith, #1982: AQS, 1989, 144 pages, softbound, $19.95
- **Gallery of American Quilts 1830-1991: Book III,** #3421: AQS, 1992, 128 pages, softbound, $19.95
- **The Grand Finale: A Quilter's Guide to Finishing Projects,** Linda Denner, #1924: AQS, 1988, 96 pages, softbound, $14.95
- **Heirloom Miniatures,** Tina M. Gravatt, #2097: AQS, 1990, 64 pages, softbound, $9.95
- **Infinite Stars,** Gayle Bong, #2283: AQS, 1992, 72 pages, softbound, $12.95
- **The Ins and Outs: Perfecting the Quilting Stitch,** Patricia J. Morris, #2120: AQS, 1990, 96 pages, softbound, $9.95
- **Irish Chain Quilts: A Workbook of Irish Chains & Related Patterns,** Joyce B. Peaden, #1906: AQS, 1988, 96 pages, softbound, $14.95
- **Jacobean Appliqué: Book I, "Exotica,"** Patricia B. Campbell & Mimi Ayars, Ph.D, #3784: AQS, 1993, 160 pages, softbound, $18.95
- **The Judge's Task: How Award-Winning Quilts Are Selected,** Patricia J. Morris, #3904: AQS, 1993, 128 pages, softbound, $19.95
- **The Log Cabin Returns to Kentucky: Quilts from the Pilgrim/Roy Collection,** Gerald Roy and Paul Pilgrim, #3329: AQS, 1992, 36 pages, 9 x 7, softbound, $12.95
- **Marbling Fabrics for Quilts: A Guide for Learning & Teaching,** Kathy Fawcett & Carol Shoaf, #2206: AQS, 1991, 72 pages, softbound, $12.95
- **More Projects and Patterns: A Second Collection of Favorite Quilts,** Judy Florence, #3330: AQS, 1992, 152 pages, softbound, $18.95
- **Nancy Crow: Quilts and Influences,** Nancy Crow, #1981: AQS, 1990, 256 pages, 9 x 12, hardcover, $29.95
- **Nancy Crow: Work in Transition,** Nancy Crow, #3331: AQS, 1992, 32 pages, 9 x 10, softbound, $12.95
- **New Jersey Quilts – 1777 to 1950: Contributions to an American Tradition,** The Heritage Quilt Project of New Jersey; text by Rachel Cochran, Rita Erickson, Natalie Hart & Barbara Schaffer, #3332: AQS, 1992, 256 pages, softbound, $29.95
- **No Dragons on My Quilt,** Jean Ray Laury with Ritva Laury & Lizabeth Laury, #2153: AQS, 1990, 52 pages, hardcover, $12.95
- **Oklahoma Heritage Quilts,** Oklahoma Quilt Heritage Project #2032: AQS, 1990, 144 pages, softbound, $19.95
- **Old Favorites in Miniature,** Tina Gravatt #3469: AQS, 1993, 104 pages, softbound, $15.95
- **A Patchwork of Pieces: An Anthology of Early Quilt Stories 1845-1940,** complied by Cuesta Ray Benberry and Carol Pinney Crabb, #3333: AQS, 1993, 360 pages, 5½ x 8½, softbound, $14.95
- **Quilt Groups Today: Who They Are, Where They Meet, What They Do, and How to Contact Them – A Complete Guide for 1992-1993,** #3308: AQS, 1992, 336 pages, softbound, $14.95
- **Quilt Registry,** Lynne Fritz, #2380: AQS, 1992, 80 pages, hardbound, $9.95
- **Quilting Patterns from Native American Designs,** Dr. Joyce Mori, #3467: AQS, 1993, 80 pages, softbound, $12.95
- **Quilting with Style: Principles for Great Pattern Design,** Gwen Marston & Joe Cunningham, #3470: AQS, 1993, 192 pages, 9 x 12, hardbound, $24.95
- **Quiltmaker's Guide: Basics & Beyond,** Carol Doak, #2284: AQS, 1992, 208 pages, softbound, $19.95
- **Quilts: Old & New, A Similar View,** Paul D. Pilgrim and Gerald E. Roy, #3715: AQS, 1993, 40 pages, softbound, $12.95
- **Quilts: The Permanent Collection – MAQS,** #2257: AQS, 1991, 100 pages, 10 x 6½, softbound, $9.95
- **Seasons of the Heart & Home: Quilts for a Winter's Day,** Jan Patek, #3796: AQS, 1993, 160 pages, softbound, $18.95
- **Seasons of the Heart & Home: Quilts for Summer Days,** Jan Patek, #3761: AQS, 1993, 160 pages, softbound, $18.95
- **Sensational Scrap Quilts,** Darra Duffy Williamson, #2357: AQS, 1992, 152 pages, softbound, $24.95
- **Sets & Borders,** Gwen Marston & Joe Cunningham, #1821: AQS, 1987, 104 pages, softbound, $14.95
- **Show Me Helen...How to Use Quilting Designs,** Helen Squire, #3375: AQS, 1993, 155 pages, softbound, $15.95
- **Somewhere in Between: Quilts and Quilters of Illinois,** Rita Barrow Barber, #1790: AQS, 1986, 78 pages, softbound, $14.95
- **Spike & Zola: Patterns for Laughter...and Appliqué, Painting, or Stenciling,** Donna French Collins, #3794: AQS, 1993, 72 pages, softbound, $9.95
- **Stenciled Quilts for Christmas,** Marie Monteith Sturmer, #2098: AQS, 1990, 104 pages, softbound, $14.95
- **Three-Dimensional Appliqué and Embroidery Embellishment: Techniques for Today's Album Quilt,** Anita Shackelford, #3788: AQS, 1993, 152 pages, 9 x 12, hardbound, $24.95
- **A Treasury of Quilting Designs,** Linda Goodmon Emery, #2029: AQS, 1990, 80 pages, 14 x 11, spiral-bound, $14.95
- **Tricks with Chintz: Using Large Prints to Add New Magic to Traditional Quilt Blocks,** Nancy S. Breland, #3847: AQS, 1994, 96 pages, softbound, $14.95
- **Wonderful Wearables: A Celebration of Creative Clothing,** Virginia Avery, #2286: AQS, 1991, 184 pages, softbound, $24.95

These books can be found in local bookstores and quilt shops. If you are unable to locate a title in your area, you can order by mail from AQS, P.O. Box 3290, Paducah, KY 42002-3290.
Please add $1 for the first book and 40¢ for each additional one to cover postage and handling.
(International orders please add $1.50 for the first book and $1 for each additional one.)